DEATH OF A TEXAS RANGER

DEATH OF A TEXAS RANGER

*A True Story of Murder and Vengeance
on the Texas Frontier*

CYNTHIA LEAL MASSEY

TWODOT®

Guilford, Connecticut
Helena, Montana
An imprint of Globe Pequot Press

To buy books in quantity for corporate use
or incentives, call **(800) 962-0973**
or e-mail **premiums@GlobePequot.com.**

A · **TWODOT**® · **BOOK**

Project editor: Lauren Szalkiewicz
Layout: Chris Mongillo

Library of Congress Cataloging-in-Publication data is available on file.

ISBN 978-0-7627-9305-1

Printed in the United States of America

10 9 8 7 6 5 4 3 2 1

Contents

Preface

While researching a history book about Helotes, Texas, a small town near San Antonio, I heard bits and pieces of a story about the murder of a sergeant in Texas Ranger Minute Men Troop V of Medina County, which mustered into service September 1, 1872. Several men from the Helotes settlement in northwest Bexar County had enlisted in the troop, composed of farmers and ranchers, to stave off Indian raids.

In the summer of 1873, after the troop had been together for almost a year, Sergeant John Green was shot and killed by a Ranger under his command in circumstances shrouded in mystery. The Ranger who killed him—Cesario Menchaca—was one of three in the troop of Mexican descent. A farmer, Menchaca had also served as a constable in the Helotes precinct.

I continued to research and ask questions, and slowly the details of the murder emerged. The more I learned about the events surrounding the shooting, the more intrigued I became. When I learned that "Old Man Marnoch"—a prominent, but eccentric, character—was involved, I was hooked.

Gabriel Wilson Marnoch, also known as G. W. Marnock (1838–1920), was the eldest son of the founding family of Helotes. An emigrant from Scotland, he became a frontier naturalist who discovered four new reptile and amphibian species in the Helotes hills and served as a field correspondent for paleontologist Professor Edward Drinker Cope. Marnoch's herpetological collections can now be found at the Smithsonian Institution in Washington, DC, and the Mayborn Museum at Baylor University. Marnoch also carried on an extensive correspondence by letter with the "Father of American Vertebrate Paleontology," Professor Joseph Leidy of the Academy of Natural Sciences in Philadelphia.

The Marnoch homestead, built in 1859, is a Texas Historic Landmark and is mostly associated with Gabriel, who lived there with his wife and children until his death.

Eighty-four-year-old Armin Eldmendorf, who taught school in Helotes in 1907, wrote in a 1974 memoir: "I inquired how to get to the Marnock [*sic*] house, as Gabriel Marnock was one of the three school trustees I had to see. The saloonkeeper warned me about Marnock and confirmed the story I had been given by the County Superintendent of Schools. Marnock, it was rumored, was an educated man who had committed two murders."

Two murders?

An exhaustive search of county criminal records and newspapers yielded the story of one murder. But further research led me from Marnoch to the tale of John Green and his killer, Cesario Menchaca.

As I delved more deeply into the story of the men and the Texas Ranger troop, I realized this was more than a story about a killing. It was the story of an era. Green's killing exemplifies the chaotic frontier society in Texas after the Civil War, a time fraught with political turmoil, cultural clashes, and a tenuous hold on life.

And yet, even amid the chaos, the virgin landscape of Texas was a magnet to those interested in the natural sciences in the nineteenth century, an era often referred to as the Age of Darwin, a nod to British naturalist Charles Darwin, who in 1859 and 1871, respectively, published his seminal scientific works, *The Origin of Species* and *The Descent of Man.*

Darwin's works espoused the theory of evolution by means of natural selection and inspired naturalists throughout the world. In Texas, those engaged in the natural sciences often had to contend with hostility and suspicion. While pioneers struggled for survival, intrepid and often eccentric men traipsed across the countryside with large hooks, snake bags, and jars filled with alcohol preservatives, into which were stuffed an assortment of wildlife. It is not hard to imagine the dismay of settlers neither scientifically inclined, nor willing to concede relation to apes.

Nevertheless, according to Samuel Wood Geiser, author of *Naturalists of the Frontier*, "several hundred men of science labored in Texas in the pioneer days." In particular, the 1870s were a time of "awakened interest in natural history in Texas," and during this decade Helotes's preeminent naturalist Gabriel Wilson Marnoch began his work in earnest.

The 1870s also saw disgruntled Indian tribes forced onto US reservations and others who fled across the Mexican border wage an escalating, frantic, but ultimately foiled crusade to regain their territory and prominence. Their bounty was horses, and they could not have chosen a more valuable commodity to steal from the Texan usurpers.

Cynthia Leal Massey
Helotes, Texas

PART ONE
1870–1880

We will now discuss in a little more detail the struggle for existence.
—Charles Darwin, The Origin of Species

I sat up many nights at my window with a blanket
and had a gun under it and I thought every minute
the Indians were coming in the yard.

—AUGUSTA BALLSCHEIT

I

Indians Were Coming

FEBRUARY 1870

John Green dozed off on the couch to the aroma of Gussie's cooking and the swish of her broom on the porch. The tension in his muscles relaxed after the long horseback ride with Jacob Hoffman. Riding through a neighbor's ranch, they'd found a dead mare pierced with arrows, pieces of flesh cut from its haunch, a sure sign that Comanches were in the area. The beginning of 1870 was proving no different from the previous years. In fact, Indian raids were increasing all over Texas.

Despite the new line of forts reinstituted along the Texas frontier a year after the end of the war and an 1867 treaty that conferred "firm title" to almost three million acres to the Indians north of the Washita River (in exchange for ninety million acres ceded to the US government), sporadic raids and killings continued. The tribes, accustomed to roaming the plains at will, did not like the aggressive military muscle used to move them onto the reservations, nor the confinement to their allotted land. They began slipping out of the reservations, and their favorite place of mayhem was Texas, the former republic.

Since the mid-1700s, the Comanches had ruled the Texas plains. Although Texas had joined the Union in 1845, the Comanches considered it a territory apart from the United States and not governed by the rules of the treaty.

Green's infant son Willie was snuggled in a quilt to keep off the chill. The babe slept peacefully in his cradle, despite the moonlight piercing through cracks in the shuttered windows of the limestone cabin.

Gussie's voice sliced through her husband's slumber. "Someone's after the horses!"

John leapt off the couch and rushed to the porch. The distant sound of hooves drummed on the dry earth. A howl broke over the steady beat.

Behind him, Gussie said, "Sounds like a hurt dog."

Groggy from sleep, John rubbed his eyes as he ran toward the gate, his wife trailing him. They heard someone riding toward them and froze.

Two Indians on horseback stopped in front of John's saddle horse, hobbled not fifteen feet from the house where he'd left it after his return from his long day in the saddle. One of the Indians jumped off his mount, slashed the hobbles, and climbed on John's horse. John ran back to the cabin, cursing himself for neglecting to grab his gun on the way out. When he returned with his rifle, the Indians—and his horse—were gone.

He and Gussie rushed over to the broken-down dun left by the raiders. It had a split ear and three marks on its thigh. "Comanche," John said.

Gussie ran back to the cabin and bolted the door shut as John pushed through the brush toward the creek and the Jacob Hoffmann homestead.

John and Jacob returned a few hours later, on foot, with the grim news that all of Jacob's horses had been stolen, as well as those of their neighbor Friedrick Braun. John Green's loss of his saddle horse was insignificant compared to Jacob's loss of forty animals and Braun's twelve.

When Gussie asked about the howls, Jacob told her the Indians had shot his dog with an arrow, and his ranch hand had "pulled it out."

The men left again, returning several hours later on saddle horses as the sun rose. Gussie met them on the porch. Jacob said they'd "sent word to the soldiers stationed in San Antonio to come and trail the Indians."

Illness prevented Braun joining the chase, but both John and Jacob left again to follow the trail. Jacob welcomed any occasion to go after Indians, perhaps in revenge for what they'd done to his older brother fourteen years earlier. While John Hoffmann worked on the roof of his cabin on the bank of the Medina River, Comanches had attacked. He'd been foolhardy to insist on building his homestead in the wilderness, but Jacob was sure his brother didn't deserve to be mutilated, scalped, and left on the ground naked, arrows shot through his head and back. This memory urged Jacob on, although his wife, nine months pregnant, was past her due date. He did ask Green to return home to look after both their families.

When Jacob returned a few days later, empty-handed, he was greeted with congratulations on the birth of a son, his fifth child. And area ranchers were eager to hear what happened on the trail. Jacob's response was later reported in a deposition in the United States Court of Claims for Indian Depredations.

We followed the trail for about 25 miles . . . and night overtook us. The Indians set the prairies on fire that night. . . . The next morning we went off the trail to get some water and when we got back on it everything was burnt up. The Lieutenant refused to go on because he had orders to only follow the trail . . .

On hearing this story, the ranchers railed against the Indians, the post soldiers, and the federal government's peace policy. Under this

1867 policy, President Grant had assigned Quaker pacifists to administer the business of the reservation tribes. The theory was that through the inculcation of Christianity and education, including the teaching of agriculture, the tribes would learn to accept a peaceful existence on their reservations.

Another part of the policy required that the Army remain passive in its dealings with the Indians. Only if the tribes were caught in an illegal or injurious act as it was being perpetrated could the Army intervene. Their orders were to escort those Indians who'd left the reservation back to the Indian Territory. They were not allowed to follow the Indians into their territory, "even in hot pursuit," and the Army could not punish Indians "without the permission of the agents, for any cause."

Texans believed that the Comanches and their allies were being coddled and protected by the US government, which had turned a blind eye to "unscrupulous traders" who sold firearms to the Indians in exchange for horses and other contraband stolen from isolated Texas ranches.

John Green had been lucky this time; the raid had cost him only one horse. But he still felt a bitter gall about the thirty-six horses the renegades had stolen a year previously, just a few days after he brought his bride to the ranch. Fine stock they were. Their sale to the Army post would have provided much needed income for his family. He knew how Jacob felt; he also knew that it was futile to depend on others—particularly the government—to protect your property and family.

He'd learned early that life in Texas was one hard blow after another. You either got up swinging, or you stayed put licking your wounds, never amounting to much.

DECEMBER 1852

Johann Gruen, the boy who would become John Green, lost both his parents by the time he was twelve. After his father's death in December

1852, he lingered on the fringes of the crowd assembled at his family's Fredericksburg, Texas, farm as the auctioneer sold off the last of his father's estate. People looked at him with pity. "Johann," they said, "your *Vater* was a good man. May he rest in peace."

But they were also ravenous for his family's belongings. The livestock were the first to go: a yoke of oxen, three cows and calves, three heifers, a horse, five hogs, eight chickens, and a rooster. The foodstuff quickly followed: forty cobs of corn, fifty pumpkins, a bucket of dry beans, and twelve pounds of salted butter. With each knock of the gavel on the makeshift table, Johann's heart fell. The sale of the household items hit him the hardest, the personal things he'd seen his *Mutter* and *Vater* use: the butter churn, the copper coffee kettle, the shovel and the hoe, his *Vater's* clothes.

When it was over, his neighbors walked away with 137 items from the house and barn that had once belonged to a fellow immigrant, who like them had come from Germany to this wilderness called Texas for a better life. While their dreams lived on, Frederick Gruen's were now as dust.

Conrad Ernst, executor of Gruen's estate, was pleased with the outcome of the auction. Johann and his siblings had made $350 from the sale. Their neighbors had been generous. Coupled with proceeds from the future sale of his father's land—640 acres from a land grant obtained through the German Emigration Company, 320 acres his father had purchased for back taxes, and the 20-acre town lot—the Gruen children were far from destitute. Yet, this knowledge, while comforting, could not ease the heartache.

Johann's mother, Catherine, had passed away two years earlier, a sad event that began the transformation of the Gruen family. His little brother Henry, barely two, had been sent to live with the widow Schmidt, the midwife who'd delivered him. That she and Henry lived on property adjacent to the Gruens' Fredericksburg town lot was little consolation.

With their father's death, Johann and his ten-year-old sister Catherine would also be parted: she to live with the Ernst family in town and on their ranch southwest of Fredericksburg near the Pedernales River; he, to the home of former Gillespie County Sheriff Louis Martin, now a stock raiser who owned a large spread on the north bank of the Llano River, forty-two miles northwest of Fredericksburg.

Since he was a child, Johann had skirted death. On his family's voyage from Germany when he was six, an infectious disease had plagued several passengers, resulting in premature death and burial at sea. Johann and his family escaped the pernicious sickness. They'd arrived at the bustling port of Galveston Island in the spring of 1846. Although a major port of entry for immigrants, the small Texas island with no bridge to the mainland was not suitable for large groups of people destined to travel inland. Like other immigrants under the auspices of the German Emigration Company, the Gruen family boarded a smaller vessel for a voyage to Indianola, a coastal town about one hundred miles southwest of Galveston.

Founded a couple of years before by the colonist commissioner Prince Carl of Solms, Germany, ostensibly because it was a more "suitable harbor" with "fresh water," Indianola had become a tent haven for more than seven thousand immigrants, stranded in part because of the war that broke out between the United States and Mexico in May 1846. The private teamsters hired by the emigration company could not resist the higher pay offered by the US Army, and left their charges to fend for themselves over the hot and mosquito-infested summer season.

As summer progressed, malaria, dysentery, and strange fevers gripped the beleaguered colonists and by the fall of 1846, "approximately 3,800 [had] died." Johann saw bodies wrapped in sheets being carried away in carts, and he heard the wails piercing through the canvas tents that populated the coastal town. Again, he, his parents, and his sister were spared.

When his family finally left Indianola in a caravan of wagons several months after their arrival, Johann had seen discarded furniture and wooden crosses along the rugged trail. He knew not to ask why they were there. He'd already begun to understand the hardships of life.

They arrived several weeks later at the settlement called Fredericksburg, a Hill Country town of well-timbered limestone hills and crystal clear rivers and streams. For a short time, life in this exotic place had been idyllic. Friendly, dark-skinned natives roamed the main street of Fredericksburg with pecans and beads to trade, often for salt and tobacco.

On hot summer days after his chores, Johann joined his friends at Baron's Creek, a stream that ran through the town. Tall grass and rushes grew along the red clay creek bank. The boys covered themselves with the clay and hid in the rushes waiting for Indians to appear.

When a group walked by, the boys would jump up and whoop and yell, "like little wild Indians." The natives laughed, and sometimes they joined the boys for a swim.

The friendly relations were the result of an 1847 treaty negotiated by the new German Emigration Company commissary general, John O. Meusebach, and Penateka Comanche chiefs Buffalo Hump, Santa Anna, and Old Owl. Meusebach knew that the land grants issued to the immigrants were worthless without cooperation from the Indians. On his side was the fact that he represented a people with whom the Comanches had no prior experience. The Comanche tribes despised the Texans and Mexicans, whom they considered interlopers and with whom they'd shared a treacherous past.

The Meusebach-Comanche treaty allowed the German settlers to travel into Indian territory unmolested and gave the same consideration to the Indians to go to the white settlements. Among other provisions, which included monetary payments to the Indians, the treaty opened to German settlement more than three million acres in the heart of the Comancheria.

Johann perhaps thought the dangers that seemed to lurk everywhere they traveled were over.

He was wrong.

In 1849, speculators passing through the German town on their
way to the gold fields in California left in their wake the seeds of a
cholera epidemic. Many settlers and several friends died that summer.
Johann soberly watched as men, bandanas covering their faces, drove
ox-drawn carts through the village to gather the bodies of the dead.

But until death touched him personally, he'd not known what it
meant to be bereft. Now, like a living thing, the word and its meaning
enveloped him.

After the auction of his father's possessions, Johann accompanied
Sheriff Martin to his new home on the Llano River, near Willow
Creek. The feather mattress and trunk filled with bed linens, towels,
and clothing—the boy's sole belongings—bumped against the side of
the wagon on the way to the Martin Ranch. John Green, as his guardian now called him, would bunk with the hands in one of the outlying
cabins on the ranch. The German-born Martin, one of the original
colonists in Fredericksburg, had taken to the frontier and the American way of life with relish. A short stocky man with a round face, he
smoked a six-inch-long pipe and carried a rifle and lariat wherever he
went. The former sheriff would not coddle his new charge.

John had heard the story of how when Martin was a boy in the old
country, he'd shot an arrow through an oil portrait of himself after he
decided the likeness was not good enough. Would he shoot an arrow
through John if the boy didn't work to his potential? John was not
willing to find out.

Martin's wife, Elizabeth, and three children under the age of five
greeted them when they arrived. John smiled at Elizabeth, the older
sister of his friend William Arhelger, who lived in Fredericksburg and
whom John had asked to watch over his younger sister and brother.
The Martins had recently moved to their new homestead, so there was

a lot of work to be done plowing, planting, and harvesting crops and tending livestock.

For the next few years on the ranch at Willow Creek, John gained knowledge of the stock-raising business. In 1856, Martin signed a contract with the US Army to supply fresh beef to several posts along the frontier. John accompanied him on freighting trips, getting a taste for the world outside the insulated German community. He became acquainted with Edwin Lane, sutler for the Second Cavalry, who supplied stores at Camp Verde, Fort Mason, and Fort McKavett, among other government posts. Known as "Stuttering Lane," the sutler had immigrated to Texas from Virginia in the early 1850s, settling in Fredericksburg. Despite his verbal affliction, Lane was considered a "clever" gentleman, as evidenced by the value of his holdings in 1860 of $4,500 in real estate and $10,000 in personal estate.

Lane had formed a partnership with fellow Virginian Bladen Mitchell, who'd started a ranch to raise horses to sell to the government posts. The ranch was on the north side of the Medina River, near a little town called Bandera, and Mitchell was looking for help.

It was a great opportunity for John Green, who had gained considerable experience during his years with Martin. By 1857, he was seventeen and had grown into a striking young man, just shy of six feet tall, slender, with guileless blue eyes and sandy hair. That year, he struck out on his own, making his way to Bandera County, a sparsely populated frontier fifty miles southwest of Fredericksburg, by way of Camp Verde.

Everybody was talking about the great camel experiment at the camp, which was ten miles north of Bandera. Secretary of State Jefferson Davis had secured appropriations to bring the beasts to Texas believing they could be used to transport dispatches and supplies between the government forts along the border and through to California. He believed camels would be more effective pack animals because they could travel longer distances and carry heavier loads than mules and horses. The federal government had selected the camp along Verde Creek as headquarters for the camels, thirty-four of which had arrived in April 1856, along with their Armenian drivers and their families.

John was eager to see the exotic animals. As he neared the camp, a fence of concrete and timber several hundred feet in length and about fifteen feet high loomed before him. His horse danced a bit and let out a loud snort. At exactly the same time, John caught a whiff of a nasty odor. He soon learned the smell's source. The fenced enclosure was the home of the camels. John had never encountered such ungainly and smelly beasts, and the soldiers being trained as handlers told him that they'd never seen more stubborn animals. The camels spit at whomever they didn't like, which was just about everybody. They also frightened the horses, a big strike against them.

John, a frontiersman whose appreciation of horses and their abilities had been strengthened through the years, was no doubt appalled at the sight of the unwieldy and unattractive beasts. The camel experiment, later chalked up as another government folly paid for by taxpayer dollars, provided fodder for stories and jokes and little else.

After seeing the camel camp, he traveled south on an ancient route through Bandera Pass, a natural gorge in the long limestone ridge separating the Medina and Guadalupe valleys. Frequent battles occurred at the pass, and John saw many animal bones and skulls strewn about. Frontier naturalist Jean Louis Berlandier, who had traveled through the area as a member of the 1828 Mexican boundary and scientific expedition, observed that "a Comanche warrior" was buried in the pass, and as was custom, natives who saw the grave left offerings of "arrows, bows, sundry weapons, enemy trophies, and the like, and even sacrifice[d] mules and horses to his shade."

Likely eager to get through the isolated and eerie valley, John picked up his pace, arriving a few hours later in Bandera, a settlement made up of a small commissary store and a few cabins along a dusty main street. However, the horse-powered sawmill on the Medina River, which ran along the southern part of the town, was a hotbed of activity. Several men worked at the mill cutting cypress trees that grew along the banks of the river. The mill supplied timber for a shingle-making business, as well as lumber sold to the San Antonio market some forty-five miles away.

In addition to the few families in the sparsely populated community, about 175 Mormons had settled twelve miles south of town on the north side of the Medina River. The Mormon camp was two miles south of Mitchell's ranch, also located on the north side of the river.

This colony of Mormons had originally settled near Fredericksburg in 1847. Not long after John's family had arrived in Fredericksburg, the sect—under the leadership of elder Lyman Wight—established a community they called Zodiac on the Pedernales a few miles southeast of town. Wight had been an early leader in the Latter Day Saints movement in Missouri. After the death of church founder Joseph Smith, the group broke into several factions, and Wight decided to lead his own group to Texas. He was excommunicated from the main church, which had reorganized in the Utah territory under the direction of Brigham Young.

The polygamous sect had built homes, a school, a temple, and a sawmill and gristmill on the Pedernales. "Although the Germans considered the Mormons to be 'lawless of religious practices,' they accepted the newcomers because they realized the need to learn the American way of milling, agriculture, and livestock," according to Sarah Kay Curtis, who in 1943, wrote her master's thesis on the history of Gillespie County.

Wight was elected chief justice of Gillespie County in the fall of 1850, after successfully challenging the qualifications of his German opponent, who was not an American citizen. His opponent had received more votes, and the German population was not happy that their majority vote was overturned. What was more, Mormons also held several other county offices and seemed to be consolidating power. The Germans instigated several special elections during 1851 that were rife with irregularities, finally taking back their supremacy. Although Wight remained chief justice, he stopped attending commissioners' court meetings. The Mormon leader decided to "have nothing more to do with Gillespie County politics," and his office was declared vacant in the summer of 1851.

Whether for that reason or the devastating February 1851 flood that ruined the mill, flooded out homes, and destroyed their cropland, the sect abandoned their settlement. They traveled around central Texas, stopping for a while in different communities until the spring of 1854, when they eventually settled in Bandera County. In the fall of that year, they moved to a more isolated location along the Medina River, establishing a village they called Mountain Valley. They constructed a horse-powered mill for "sawing and grinding," and began making furniture for sale, among other economic endeavors.

What John thought of the Mormons is unknown, but as a baptized and confirmed Lutheran, he likely respected their industry, yet had the same unsettled feeling about the sect as did his German compatriots. A year after John's 1857 arrival in Bandera, Mormon leader Wight had a fatal seizure while traveling on a road near San Antonio. His colony broke up, although several families remained in Bandera County.

SPRING 1857

Bladen Mitchell welcomed John to his ranch on the banks of the lower Medina River and set him to work from sunrise to sunset gathering horses, moving them from one pasture or corral to another, breaking broncos, and branding colts. Five years older than his new employee, the ranch owner was a "genial" man. Average in size, with dark thinning hair and a neatly trimmed beard and mustache, he was a southerner to the core, known for his manners and hospitality. Eager for land and opportunity, Mitchell had emigrated from Manassas, Virginia, to Texas in about 1854.

Mitchell's ranch was a fine grazing range for horses. Gamma and buffalo grass and wild rye grew on the prairies surrounded by gently sloping hills. Along the river were varieties of oak, as well as pecan and cypress trees. Wild game was abundant, and food easily secured. However, Mitchell's cowboys had to be ever watchful for panthers and feral hogs that could rip a horse to shreds in minutes.

John Green also had to face another hard fact about life away from the German community in which he was raised—the constant threat of Indian raids. "Between 1836 and 1860, an average of about two hundred men, women, and children were killed or carried off each year," wrote T. R. Fehrenbach, in his seminal *Lone Star: A History of Texas and the Texans*. Adding to that grim statistic was the valuable chattel of horses and cattle, thousands of which the Indians stole not only for themselves but also for trade.

Federal Indian agents believed that guaranteeing Indian land rights was the key to peace, but state officials would not approve public lands for Indian reservations within the state. Nevertheless, in 1854, the Texas Legislature relented and approved the allocation of land for two small reservations comprising a total of 37,000 acres on the Brazos. Unfortunately, when raids occurred, it was the Indians from these reservations who were blamed "for either conducting or abetting them." White settlers retaliated against the reservation Indians regardless of guilt or innocence.

Throughout the 1850s, new settlers continued to push their way into the Comancheria, plowing under valuable Indian hunting grounds and grazing ranges. By 1858, just a few Comanche bands still existed, and those that had refused to be confined on the reservations struck back against the Texan interlopers with brutal raids.

In several raids on the Mormon colony just two miles south of Mitchell's ranch, Indians stole almost all of the group's livestock. In a letter to the local federal Indian agent, Wight wrote that the "Comanches had stolen sixteen horses and twenty-five oxen, as well as butchered two steers." He wanted military protection. However, the agent, Major Robert Neighbors, had pro-Indian sympathies (which instigated his murder in 1859) and offered no aid.

In a March 7, 1856, letter to the Texas governor, Wight wrote that the "Indians had stolen $3,000 of his stock since 1851," and had just taken the last of his horses, "which put idle his grist mill, sawmill, and turning lathe." He had no more money to purchase horses and asked for help. Again Wight was rebuffed. There would be no financial help, although the governor said he'd dispatch "a few Rangers."

When Indians stole stock from Mitchell's ranch, John and his fellow ranch hands formed a posse to go after them. He learned how to track and never flinched from a fight. Locals believed him to be "one of the bravest and best Indian fighters on this frontier." By 1859, having proved his mettle, he became ranch foreman, chosen not simply for his Indian fighting skills, but also for his calm temperament as demonstrated in the following anecdote related fifty-one years later in *A Texas Pioneer* by August Santleban.

On a Monday afternoon in 1859, fourteen-year-old Santleban galloped toward Green at full speed. As the boy got closer, John recognized him. At the time, August often made mail deliveries between his father's ranch in Castroville and Bandera.

August jumped off his mount, gulping and spitting out words: "Injuns. Six miles south. Kilt."

John grabbed the boy's shoulders. "Calm down, and tell me what happened."

The boy took a deep breath. "We took a wrong trail about six miles back."

"We?"

"Me and another boy, a cousin to John Adamietz. He wanted a ride back to Bandera. I think they kilt him."

"Who?"

"Injuns. Saw a bunch of 'em and one of 'em shot at him and he fell off my horse, and I just took off. I was scairt. We gotta do somethin'. Put out the alarm."

"My hands are out with the horses now. When they come back, I'll send one back with you to Bandera. For right now, you gotta calm down." John walked to the well and brought up a bucket of water, offering a dipper to the boy.

As the boy gulped the water, John noticed movement in the thicket in the southern portion of the ranch from where August had emerged. Several men sprang into view.

Touching the pistol at his hip, glancing at his rifle nearby, John watched as the men—Mexicans, not Indians—neared. With them was a boy about the same age as August. "Is that your friend?" he said, glancing at August.

The boy's eyes widened as he nodded.

"Hola, Señor Green," said one of the Mexicans as he approached John. "We were out threshing pecan trees to gather nuts when the boys saw us. We realized they thought we were *indios* and that is why we are here." He gestured toward the boy whom August had left for dead. "As you can see, he is fine and there are no Indians around, only us."

John thanked the men for their quick arrival to explain the situation. They all had a good laugh, and soon the embarrassed mail carrier was on his way to Bandera, passenger in tow.

NOVEMBER 1860

Texas was culturally Southern, composed of a majority of immigrants from "the old South," who began arriving in 1835 and continued their migration until the onset of the Civil War. A slave state, its primary industry was agriculture, "with cotton planters and Negroes in the eastern regions, [and] a surly, sturdy horde of small corn farmers in the west."

By the mid-nineteenth century, slavery had become a powder keg of disagreement and moral outrage. However, in Texas, as in the other Southern states that exploited "the peculiar institution," emancipation was "economically unreasonable." The assessed value of all slaves in Texas was 20 percent more than the assessed value of all the state's cultivated lands. Nevertheless, slavery as an institution was not popular among all groups in Texas, where only 5 percent of the population owned slaves. However, most white Texas farmers considered Negroes inferior and were adamantly against the idea of their equality. A majority of German immigrants who considered slavery "evil" and incompatible with the "foundation of democracy" were the exception.

After white abolitionist John Brown attempted to seize a US arsenal in Harpers Ferry, Virginia, on October 16, 1859, along with thirteen white and five Negroes supporters, with the intent to lead a mass insurrection against slavery, Texans went into a collective panic. Those who'd ever spoken in favor of the abolition of slavery or even advocated humane treatment of slaves got their comeuppance: arson, floggings, hangings, and public book burnings, though not widespread, were nonetheless serious reminders that dissent would not be tolerated.

When Abraham Lincoln, who'd made known his antipathy for slavery and who got zero votes in Texas, won the presidency on November 8, 1860, talk of secession ratcheted up among the slave states. Two months later, South Carolina was the first southern state to pass articles of secession. On February 1, 1861, delegates from Texas counties who'd been sent to the special convention to debate secession voted 166 to 8 for an Ordinance of Secession, and on February 23, Texans voted for the referendum to secede by a vote of 46,188 to 15,149, making Texas the seventh state to leave the Union.

Gillespie County, where John Green had grown up, voted overwhelmingly against secession, while Bandera County, where he was then living, voted for secession by a slim majority of one vote—thirty-three to thirty-two. Gillespie County had a German population of about 80 percent, while Bandera County was just 20 percent culturally German. According to Levi Lamoni Wight, a son of the deceased Mormon leader, "We [the former Wightites] took largely of the spirit of rebellion." With a sizeable voting bloc, the Mormon community likely pushed the vote in favor of secession.

Those Germans against secession had come from war-torn countries and were not eager to get involved in another bloody battle. They supported Lincoln and Texas Governor Sam Houston, who'd wanted no part of secession and who was later evicted from office for refusing to take an oath of loyalty to the Confederacy. While John may have agreed with his German compatriots, the times dictated a pragmatic approach to the irrational politics of the era. Ultimately, a majority of Texans gave their allegiance to the Confederacy and most able-bodied men enlisted to fight.

When a call to service was announced, "the response, by any historical standard, was phenomenal." Although only twenty companies were requested for service in Virginia, thirty-two were formed. However, the majority of Texas's troops fought west of the Mississippi. Troops that had guarded frontier forts were redeployed elsewhere, leaving isolated settlements vulnerable. In December 1861, the state authorized the creation of Frontier Regiments, not considered part of the Confederate Forces, to protect settlers on the Texas frontier against marauding Indians and Mexican bandits, advertising for men from frontier counties "who presented themselves for service with good horses and proper arms . . . [and] who were Indian fighters."

John saddled his horse and rode from Mitchell's ranch to Bandera on February 17, 1862, to enlist as a private in Company D Frontier Regiment, under the command of Captain Charles de Montel. The forty-eight-year-old captain owned more than thirty thousand acres; in spite of his German heritage, he also owned nine slaves and had been a delegate who voted in favor of secession. A respected lawyer and land surveyor from Castroville, he'd assisted in platting the town site of Bandera and owned the sawmill that employed Polish immigrants, the first permanent settlers of the town.

De Montel's company, organized as ranging units, comprised 128 men from Bandera, Blanco, Kerr, Medina, and Uvalde counties. Half were stationed at Camp Verde in Kerr County, the other half at Camp Montel at the head of Seco Creek, in Bandera County. Scouts patrolled back and forth from their camps at two-day intervals, their presence designed "to act as a cordon of protection against Indian attacks on settlements."

However, Indians were not the only threat in the frontier counties. Three months after John joined the Frontier Forces, Confederate troops marched into his hometown of Fredericksburg arresting citizens and burning farms of people they believed were pro-Union; the troops rode throughout Gillespie and surrounding counties intimidating and harassing residents.

In August 1862, a Confederate cavalry troop killed fifty Hill Country Germans—alleged draft dodgers—who'd encamped along the Nueces River en route to Mexico. Those not killed during the surprise attack were murdered after being taken prisoner, and many were left unburied. This massacre, which ignited riots in San Antonio and other Hill Country counties, was universally condemned "as one of the blackest days in the history of the Confederacy."

All nine Frontier Regiments were mustered out of service after one year due to lack of funds. After his February 9, 1863, discharge from his regiment, John returned to Mitchell's ranch and joined the Bandera Home Guard, a volunteer company formed at the onset of the war "to defend the neighborhood from the wild Indians and to keep down the disorderly element at home." The Confederate Congress passed a conscription law in April 1862. To minimize the effect of the draft, believed by Texans to be a violation of state's rights, the Texas Legislature organized a new structure dividing Texas into three frontier districts under Confederate military command in December 1863. Mitchell was instituted as a captain in a troop for the Third

Frontier District. John enlisted in the troop of fifty-three men from Bandera County on February 6, 1864. In addition to stopping Indian and Mexican marauders, the frontier troop was directed to enforce conscription and arrest deserters.

In the waning days of the war, Mitchell's troop camped near the headwaters of the Llano. José Policarpo Rodríguez, a famed pioneer guide, surveyor, and Indian fighter, was in the troop in which Green served. Several years later, Rodríguez shared the following story about one of the troop's expeditions.

They'd been following an Indian trail, but as dusk fell, they settled down for the night. Not long after, a man staggered into camp. "He was a fearful-looking object; barely able to walk . . . nothing but skin and bones," Rodríguez recalled.

The troop rushed to help him to the ground, gathering around him.

"There was three of us," he said, his voice barely audible. "We deserted the Confederate service out west. We was traveling together when we came to an Indian camp. They fired on us. Kilt one. Me and the other, we ran into the brush and escaped. Been wandering around for nine days. Had nothing to eat but two young crows we found in a nest. We was so hungry, we ate 'em raw."

"Where's the other?" Captain Mitchell looked into the distance.

"Two miles back, under a bluff. Too weak to walk."

The captain ordered a party of men to find the man and bring him back to camp. Several hours later, they returned with another emaciated deserter.

They were "ravenous as wild animals," so the captain ordered a guard over them to keep them from killing themselves by overeating.

After three days, they were able to eat normally and began to gain strength. When they'd recovered, Captain Mitchell turned the deserters over to Confederate authorities.

The war was officially over April 9, 1865, with Lee's surrender at Appomattox, Virginia. Nevertheless, communication of this seminal event to Texas was slow. A Union colonel who'd arrived in Brownsville during a truce established to await the outcome of the Grant-Lee meeting instigated what would be the last battle of the Civil War. Ignoring the truce, on May 12, 1865, he ordered his Negro regiment to fight. The battle, fought on the banks of the Rio Grande and called the Battle of Palmito Ranch, ended the next day in a hollow Confederate "victory."

MAY 1865

John traveled to Fredericksburg to attend his sister's wedding on May 14, 1865. Catherine Gruen had been betrothed to William Arhelger for five years. John often joked that when he'd asked his friend all those years earlier to watch over his younger sister, he didn't mean that William had to marry her. Actually, he couldn't have been more pleased. William, who'd apprenticed as a wheelwright in Boerne, was ready to set up shop in Fredericksburg and would be able to provide the love and support Catherine deserved.

The wedding celebration was bittersweet; the years of war had taken their toll. Indians had killed William's older brother Henry in 1863; William's brother-in-law and John's former guardian, Louis Martin, had been murdered a year later on a freighting trip to Mexico while transporting cotton. Nevertheless, that day in May the focus was on the bride and groom. And, perhaps, for John, on a young lady named Augusta Specht, the pretty sixteen-year-old daughter of Fredericksburg's first postmaster.

John had known the Specht family all his life; along with the Gruens, they had been among the first German families to settle in Fredericksburg. Augusta's father Theodore had been appointed the town's first postmaster in 1848. He opened a store, which also served as the post office, and as a youth John had often bought candy at the Specht commissary. But he had hardly noticed Augusta, who was eight years his junior. And, of course, he'd been away from Fredericksburg for a long time. But little Gussie had grown up, as he now noticed.

Theodore had died in 1862, leaving wife Maria and seven children, the youngest just two months old. As the eldest child, the fatherless Augusta surely had much responsibility in the Specht home, but not so much work that she would miss a neighbor's wedding.

Augusta had dark hair that framed a finely proportioned face, a delicate nose, and lips perhaps a bit thin, but which turned into a smile more often than not. She had an effervescent personality, and John, more reserved, was powerfully attracted to her.

They carried on a long-distance courtship while John focused his attention on the business of breeding and raising horses, with the intent to save money to be able to support a wife, a difficult endeavor given the state of affairs after the war. The country was in chaos. The state had been put under military rule and Texans chafed under it. Frontier communities had to fend for themselves and the Comanches took full advantage of the situation. According to a deposition made by Green on September 15, 1866, "he went out to look for his horses, and about two miles from his house met with 7 Indjans [sic], 5 of them pursued him about a mile, at [the] same time they took nine of his riding horses" valued at $900. He also noted "that the same Indjans [sic] kill[ed] and took 15 head of caviard horses belong to Bladen Mitchell and E[dwin] Lane," valued at $375.

The Indians made such frequent raids on Mitchell's ranch during that era that the owner gave up horse raising, turning his attention to cattle, which did not require the intensive effort involved in breeding and raising horses. When his employers, now including Edwin Lane who'd gone into business with Mitchell, ran short of cash to pay John his salary, they instead gave him the last of their saddle horses in payment. Many of them had been sired by a stallion of "very fine blood." John, who'd never recovered the nine horses stolen in the 1866 Indian raid, was happy to accept the payment. Local ranchers wanted colts descended from that stallion, and so Green was able to start a lucrative horse-raising business, which finally put him in a position to wed.

Three years after his sister's wedding to William Arhelger, John married Augusta Specht in an evening wedding ceremony in Fredericksburg on December 28, 1868. They began their life together on a hundred-acre spread John had purchased a few months before in a settlement called Helotes.

January 1869

Helotes, John told Augusta, meant "ears of corn." Indians had once lived along the loamy banks of the twelve-mile long Helotes Creek and cultivated the grain. As the couple made their way toward the limestone cabin in a clearing near the creek, they surveyed the fine herd of horses grazing in the pasture as the wagon, laden with their belongings, lumbered along.

The couple had left their hometown two weeks after their wedding, when the full moon had waned. Traveling in darkness would offer less temptation to renegades. Even so, John never let his guard down. He was a frontiersman, through and through. The hoot of an owl—a typical Indian signal—the whoosh of the wind, the falling of rocks kept him reaching for his rifle.

The seventy-mile ride from Fredericksburg took more than a week in the coldest month of the year. But new bride Augusta "Gussie" was hardy, like most Texas natives, and used to extremes of weather: summer heat that could fry an egg; winter northers that sliced a body like a knife.

Along the way, John shared information about their new home. Helotes was a settlement of farms and ranches spread apart, mostly homestead grants of 160 acres and larger. Mexicans lived in the northern part of the settlement, Germans in the south. There was no town center, except for Mueller's place, where the German blacksmith supplied horses for stages. And the big town of San Antonio was just a day's ride by horseback, about twenty miles southeast as the crow flies.

John told Gussie about their nearest neighbors, the Hoffmanns. He'd bought his hundred acres from Jacob Hoffmann. They'd known each other since John's days at Mitchell's ranch in Bandera. John had built their cabin across the creek from Jacob's place, so when he was away, Augusta could call on the Hoffmanns when she needed help, and, of course, having a woman friend around was a blessing on the frontier. Jacob and his wife, Carolina, had been married five years and already had four children, the youngest just six months old.

The conversation helped pass the time as they traveled on the packed dirt road through expansive valleys amid hills dotted with spindly oaks and junipers, evergreen against the yellow and brown landscape. Their route led them from Fredericksburg to the settlement of Comfort, to Boerne, to the hamlet of Leon Springs, and then down the stage road to Helotes.

On the rutted stage route that followed the north leg of Helotes Creek, they passed a stately two-story limestone house in a clearing. The Marnochs lived there, John told Gussie. They were a Scottish family with more than fifteen hundred acres. The eldest son, Gabriel, often passed his time along the creek looking for frogs and lizards and such.

Perhaps Augusta felt an affinity toward Gabriel Marnoch upon hearing this revelation. Her father had also been interested in the natural sciences. A collector of insects, lizards, and snakes, Theodore Specht had shipped several specimen collections from Fredericksburg to naturalists in New York over the years before his death in 1862, sending the money he earned from the transactions to his mother in Germany.

If Augusta's impression of Marnoch was initially favorable, it would be sorely tested in the years to come.

When they'd reached the Green homestead, Gussie admired the thirty-six horses—saddle horses, mares and their colts, and yearlings—that grazed near her new home. John bred them, the finest horses in the county, and sold them to the government.

In four days they would be gone, stolen by Indians.

But I was born a Scotchman, and a bare one, and was therefore born to fight my way with my left hand where my right failed me, and with my teeth, if they were both cut off.

—Sir Walter Scott

2

Born a Scotchman

September 1858

When the ruddy-faced Scotsman jumped out of the stagecoach in San Antonio's Main Plaza in the fall of 1858, passersby gawked. While they were used to seeing "strange faces . . . at every corner," this young man was unusual. He was tall and lanky, his legs like stilts, accentuated by a short torso. His large ears protruded from a thin, angular face. He was twenty, the age at which people say, "he'll grow into his own."

Gabriel Marnoch brushed the dust off his suit as his father, Dr. George Frederick Marnoch, fifty-five, a refined version of his son, emerged from the coach. The five-day trip from the port of Indianola to this bustling frontier town of about eight thousand had been taxing, the stage stops along the way little more than hovels with flea-infested beds. Nevertheless, their arrival in San Antonio, called by one local newspaper "the place, for capitalists, mechanics, laborers—indeed, for all classes but loafers," erased ill memories of the trip.

The Scotsmen heard German and Spanish, as well as unusual English dialects, spoken as they made their way to the nearest boardinghouse through the throng of wagons that crowded the plaza—some laden with produce, others empty, waiting for a load to transport.

The town, a mixture of dilapidated flat-roofed adobe houses and two-story limestone buildings with wrought iron porch railings, appeared to be in a state of renewal with new construction on several lots. On the west side of the plaza, a large stone church with a belfry and dome stood in disrepair. Nevertheless, women with lace veils over their heads and men, hats in hand, made the sign of the cross as they entered and exited its wooden doors. Gabriel noticed the young women, their complexions like brown sugar, dark hair long and luxurious beneath the lacy veils, very different from the pale lasses he'd grown up with.

Next to the church was an auction house, a wooden structure with a broad veranda. On the east side were several one- and two-story buildings that housed businesses and stores selling dry goods, groceries, and other merchandise. A two-story boarding house—the Plaza House—well situated on the north side of the plaza, beckoned.

Locals eagerly imparted information to the new arrivals, greenhorns, judging from their heavy Scottish brogues: *The newspapers will tell ya things are nice and peaceable these days,* they confided. *But don't let yer guard down. Horse thieves and bandits are just waitin' for people to get comfortable. A few months back, some vigilantes hanged four Meskin horse thieves out at one of the missions. Indians are everywhere in the outlying areas. And don't depend on the government post here—the soldiers never make it on time—so watch yer back.*

With these admonitions to ponder, Gabriel and his father settled into their new environs—this exotic place so different from Edinburgh, an ancient city of tall, several-story buildings, with a population in the 1850s of more than 150,000. They tended at once to the business for which they had come: purchasing land, which could be "bought at very reasonable rates." With the rest of Gabriel's family—his mother Elizabeth, and siblings Elizabeth, John, Mary Ann, and George—waiting in Boston, where they'd arrived several months before from Liverpool, he and his father had no time to waste.

Gabriel accompanied his father on visits to land agents, like one whose business on Main Plaza advertised, "Lands, City Lots, Negroes, Mules, or Other Property." As they met with various merchants and other leaders, such as the recently elected district surveyor Francois Giraud, they spread the news that the elder Marnoch was a wealthy surgeon from abroad with liquid capital who was willing to provide lending services to those with appropriate collateral. With only one chartered bank in Texas at the time—in Galveston—private lenders were in high demand.

On the first of October 1858, Gabriel and his father walked from Main Plaza to the county courthouse in the adjoining Military Plaza. The aroma of fresh coffee and meat and beans cooking on pans over wood fires welcomed them as they made their way through the bustling plaza. Surrounded by one-story adobe buildings and old Mexican huts, the plaza had the aura of a Mexican market, and was teeming with donkey-led wagons carrying cargos of produce, hay, wood, and grains. On the eastern side of the plaza food vendors dished up Mexican cuisine. A sprawling adobe building on the west side had once been the residence of governors and military commanders, hence the plaza's name. The men saw three large shade trees in front of a house from which a priest emerged, making his way across the plaza to the back of the church they now knew was called San Fernando. They passed the county jail, surrounded by a high stone wall topped by broken glass pointing skyward and cemented by mortar, promising a painful exit for inmates attempting escape.

Gabriel and his father entered the city clerk's office on the first floor of the adjoining two-story courthouse to sign documents for their first loan. The courthouse was known to locals as "the bat cave," and the Marnochs, upon hearing a commotion above their heads, soon learned why. Curious, they walked outside and followed the noise up the stairway on the side of the courthouse. They arrived at the second floor district courtroom to witness the spectacle of two bailiffs, large poles in hand, striking the canvas ceiling in preparation for a hearing. They heard a large swoosh as thousands of bats flew from the rafters under the eaves of the courthouse roof, which had become a roosting place for the winged creatures, a condition for which there seemed to be no remedy other than the aforementioned poles. Gabriel, who had an avid interest in the natural sciences, was likely intrigued, if not delighted, by the bats and their unusual habitat.

After the flight of the bats, the Marnochs returned to the clerk's office. With his son serving as his trustee, Dr. Marnoch made his first loan of $1,100 at 12 percent interest per annum to a local man, who used as collateral his lot on Martin Street in downtown San Antonio. This was the first of several loans of a thousand dollars and more that Marnoch made during the next two years, with Gabriel as his trustee. Considering that land could be purchased at one to three dollars an acre and the monthly rent for a four-room flat was about four dollars and fifty cents, this was a princely sum. Indeed, Marnoch could live off the interest alone.

A graduate of the Royal College of Surgeons in Edinburgh, Dr. Marnoch would have been warmly accepted into San Antonio's elite society, but he was not interested in the hustle and bustle of city life; he'd moved to Texas because of a "lung ailment," worsened by his time in England, where he had lived with his family before embarking on this new adventure. The death of his thirteen-year-old daughter Margaret two years before also weighed heavily on his heart. He needed respite from the constant reminder of her in England, where she had died and was buried. He was also looking forward to pursuing a new line of work. He wanted to be a cattleman and was well situated financially to be able to purchase a herd.

Francois Giraud, the surveyor, offered to show the doctor and his son several hundred acres he owned in the northwest part of the county, an area known by the name of a clear running creek that ran through it—the Helotes. It was a day's ride by horseback from San Antonio.

When Dr. Marnoch saw the gently rolling hills and valleys, he said it reminded him of Scotland. Gabriel's memories reached back to the village of Keswick in England's Lake District, a recent place of residence. While not nearly as impressive as Keswick, with its verdant valleys, shimmering crystal lakes, and snow-topped mountain ranges, the Helotes hills had an interesting topography, and the nearby creek promised a fertile and virgin territory for scientific exploration.

On October 5, Marnoch purchased the property from Giraud —1,515 acres for $1,393.75. That same day, Gabriel read with interest an article in the local newspaper about a comet that had appeared the past several nights. Gabriel and his father had joined others in the plaza craning their necks to peer at the sky. The comet would be brighter in subsequent evenings as it neared the earth.

The article, which mentioned the times past when comets produced terror in people, but which now, "in this enlightened age," prompted "speculations upon the subject matter of comets," did much to placate Gabriel, who considered himself a man of science and who must have felt out of place in this frontier town full of yokels.

Dr. Marnoch set about finding a builder for the family homestead. He'd visited Alamo Plaza upon arrival in the city. A first-class, two-story, cut-stone hotel was being erected next to the Alamo mission, now being used as a government warehouse for hay, grain, and other supplies. Mexican huts with thatched roofs huddled around the dusty plaza.

He inquired about the owner of the hotel—an expansion of a boardinghouse—and was directed to William Menger and his architect, recently elected county commissioner John M. Fries. An immigrant from Bavaria, Fries was an expert stonemason who'd built the town's Market House and had served as a contractor for the construction of the State House in Austin. Fries told Marnoch that his work on the Menger Hotel would keep him occupied until early 1859.

Marnoch was willing to wait, and while Fries finished his project, Marnoch focused on his plans for the house. It must be substantial, made of limestone quarried from the nearby hills; it must be two stories with an attic, and include an inside center stairwell. It was to have central fireplaces, like buildings in old Scotland, rather than chimneys on the exterior walls. From England, he ordered long-leaf yellow pine for the floor, mahogany for the stairway railing and double balustrade, and embossed metal ceiling tile.

During the time Marnoch was working on his house plan, William Menger came to him for a loan. His two-story, fifty-room hotel had stretched his budget beyond what he'd anticipated. Marnoch was happy to help out, if only to hasten the hotel's completion so the stonemason could commence work on Marnoch's project. On December 16, Marnoch lent Menger $2,300, again at 12 percent interest per annum, the minimum rate at the time.

By the end of January 1859, the Menger Hotel was finished. On January 24, Fries and Marnoch signed the building contract for the Marnoch homestead. Several days later, they all celebrated at the hotel's grand opening, joining a large turnout of citizens, "all seeming disposed to applaud the enterprising proprietor for the liberality displayed by him in the erection and fitting out of a hotel that would be no discredit to any city of the Union, as well as to assist him in getting through with some of his sparkling wines and incomparable lagers."

Fries took his construction team to the Helotes hills and commenced work on his new project, which, according to the contract, would be completed by March 20, barring delay in "furnishing of lumber or carpenter work." Marnoch arranged for his wife and other children to join them.

A delay did occur, not an unusual occurrence in homebuilding, but what raised the doctor's ire was not the delay but a one-hundred-dollar bill for extra work that Fries gave him in early April. Knowing the house was nearing completion, the doctor refrained from confronting

Fries; he paid three invoices in the interim, the final on April 27. In the meantime, he stewed over the bill for cut stones over the front door and second-story windows and two cut stone chimneys.

After he paid the final bill, Marnoch told Fries he would not pay the bill for extra work. There was no provision for extra work or labor in the contract, he said, so Fries had done the extra work "at his own risk." Fries, likely astonished that the wealthy surgeon would squabble over one hundred dollars, tried to reason with Marnoch, to no avail. A little over a month after the house was completed, a constable served a subpoena to Marnoch. Fries was suing him.

Marnoch had a formidable adversary in Fries, who had lived in San Antonio for twelve years and who, as an elected official, had a wide acquaintance among the town's elite. Nevertheless, what Marnoch lacked in relationships, he more than made up for in gumption.

The John Fries vs. G. F. Marnoch case went to trial in early June. The jury awarded one hundred dollars to Fries, which Marnoch appealed, directing his attorney to ask for a review of the case by another court. The review was granted. The case dragged on until the spring of 1860. By this time, Marnoch's wife and children had arrived in Texas, and the family had settled into the Marnoch homestead.

Undeterred by the nuisance lawsuit, Marnoch purchased 150 cattle in the fall of 1859, and in early April 1860, along with Gabriel, registered two brands in the Bexar District brand book. Dr. Marnoch, who had purchased stock from a man named Bracht, registered the former owner's brand, a cursive B, as his own. Gabriel registered an original brand, a stylized M.

The judge who reviewed the disputed bill case granted a new trial, which commenced on April 21, 1860. After the bats vacated the Honorable Thomas J. Devine's district court chambers, Marnoch's attorney, Albert Dittmar, laid out a case replete with architectural terms and mathematical equations that flummoxed the opposition and bemused the jury. The first piece of evidence was an affidavit from the foreman of the first jury who said he'd not been given pertinent information during the trial, such as the fact that the builder had used less rock in the building than Marnoch had purchased.

The final measurement of finished perches was less than the contract stipulated, according to Marnoch's attorney. Perches were the standard of measure for stonework: Sixteen and a half feet long, eighteen inches high, and twelve inches thick, or twenty-four and three-quarters cubic feet. Their expert witness, Mr. Giraud, measured the finished perches, which he calculated totaled 354, while Dr. Marnoch had paid for 380 perches. Dittmar concluded that Fries owed Marnoch a hundred dollars for overpayment.

To further his case against Fries, Marnoch added, "Mr. Fries warranted that the chimneys in the house would not smoke . . . but the said warranty hath wholly failed, and been violated. The chimneys smoke badly. I will have to correct them at a cost of five dollars each, twenty dollars upon the whole."

Marnoch also believed that Fries had "substituted lintels for arches in the doors and windows for his greater ease and convenience," for a loss to Marnoch of at least fifty dollars.

Swayed by the new testimony, the jury awarded Fries $37.25, considerably less than the hundred dollars he was seeking. Not happy with the verdict, Fries asked for a new trial. His motion was overruled. The verdict stood.

Marnoch's attorney fees undoubtedly exceeded the hundred dollars for which Fries sued. But that was not the issue. Marnoch not only suffered from what Scots call "short arms and deep pockets," he was also an intellectual descendant of eighteenth-century Scottish Enlightenment leaders Lord Henry Kames, a renowned legal mind, and Francis Hutchenson, a clergyman and teacher, whose most famous pupil, Adam Smith, galvanized the study of economics. Marnoch believed in the legal system and in a righteous cause. That he had the money to back up his convictions was another result of his Scottish upbringing—education and hard work. Besides these attributes, Marnoch brought with him an attitude of defiance against perceived wrongs and a willingness to fight.

Gabriel Marnoch, a witness at the trial, watched and learned.

Spring 1860

While Gabriel's father was engrossed in business and legal endeavors with his eldest son often at his side, Gabriel was immersed in a book by one of his father's schoolmates, renowned naturalist Charles Darwin. The book, *On the Origin of Species by Means of Natural Selection, or the Preservation of Favoured Races in the Struggle for Life*, destined to cause a controversy that would continue into subsequent centuries, was an immediate bestseller in England upon its November 24, 1859, publication, selling out on the first day of its release. An American reprint of the book, which cost $1.25, was available by February of 1860.

At sixteen, Darwin, son of a British doctor, had registered for medical courses at the University of Edinburgh in October 1825, the same year twenty-two-year-old George Marnoch was in attendance. While Marnoch matriculated to the Royal College of Surgeons, receiving his license to practice medicine on April 21, 1826, Darwin spent another year at the university and discovered that he was "repulsed by surgery," but had a keen interest in zoology.

Dr. Marnoch was no doubt acquainted with Darwin and may have even shared a class with him. Gabriel mentioned the renowned naturalist many years later during a dinner conversation with a prospective teacher of a school for which Gabriel served as a trustee, saying that he had had "considerable correspondence" with Darwin and fellow naturalist Thomas Huxley, although said letters have yet to surface.

While Dr. Marnoch was intent upon learning the cattle business, Gabriel, inspired by Darwin's new theory of evolutionary descent through natural selection, was more interested in roaming the hills, caves, and creek beds in search of new species of vertebrates. Nevertheless, he could not devote much time to his avocation. For the next several years, he worked alongside his father to establish a prosperous family ranch in the Helotes hills.

The Civil War halted the expansion of Dr. Marnoch's cattle enterprise. No doubt he offered his services as a physician, not only to those who returned wounded, but also to those who remained behind. Marnoch was a physician, surgeon, and apothecary, the type of doctor the Edinburgh school produced. He was a hands-on generalist who could make a diagnosis and apply the treatment himself. He was also learned in the field of obstetrics, which had become a medical discipline in the early eighteenth century.

Midwives delivered the vast majority of children in nineteenth-century Texas. However, one frigid day in January 1862, a neighbor knocked upon Dr. Marnoch's door and entreated him to come to his ranch. His wife was in labor. Family lore says that Gabriel, then twenty-four, accompanied his father to the home of Pedro and Manuela Treviño and assisted in the delivery of their first child, Carmel, who twenty years later became Gabriel's wife.

Dr. Marnoch also became involved in the cotton trade during the war, likely for a dual purpose: to keep sons Gabriel and John out of battle and to capitalize on a lucrative endeavor that would benefit his family firstly, and the Confederacy tangentially. It is unlikely the Marnochs were ardent supporters of the Confederacy, but Texas was a Confederate State. Their Scottish practicality would have compelled their actions. They became exporters of cotton from San Antonio to Mexico, with Dr. Marnoch as the financier and Gabriel as his "duly authorized agent."

Texas's common border with Mexico allowed for cotton to be shipped across the Rio Grande and transported to Mexican coastal ports, where it could be sold to merchants in "foreign vessels bound for European markets in exchange for necessary war materials such as Enfield rifles, ammunition, and percussion caps."

The cotton business, however, was not without risks. Traders had to contend with bandits on both sides of the border. During one of Gabriel's trips, Kickapoos attacked his caravan of fourteen wagons, mistaking it for another party "that had done them some injury." Marnoch and his team captured a Kickapoo whose leg had been broken during the ensuing fight, mended his injury, and took the Indian with them as they continued on to port. The Indian, who "proved very trustworthy," accompanied Marnoch on his cotton trading trips for the duration of the war.

At the end of the war, Dr. Marnoch sold most of his stock of cattle to local rancher Jacob Hoffmann. Perhaps the doctor's venture into the cotton trade, a less laborious and more profitable endeavor than running cattle, influenced his decision.

In 1867, Dr. Marnoch and sons were accused of "fraudulently embezzling" eleven thousand pounds of cotton worth $3,520 and were sued. Gabriel's mother died the same year, and as the lawsuit progressed through various legal proceedings, his father passed away in 1870.

At age thirty-one, Gabriel became head of the family. Although he'd have more responsibilities, his new position would also allow him more freedom to spend time in the field. It also unleashed something else within the budding naturalist—his irascible temperament.

NOVEMBER 1871

Carrying his rifle, hook, and pouch crammed with jars, Gabriel most often traipsed through the hills behind his home, but one cold November day in 1871, he ventured to the creek, a virtual laboratory of exotic critters. He made his way across the field in front of the homestead, crushing frost on the loamy soil. He gripped his rifle, ready in case of an encounter with a thieving Comanche or the law.

Although some believed that Kickapoos marauding from Mexico had been stealing livestock from the settlement for several years, Marnoch said in an Indian depredation deposition that the raiders in the Helotes settlement "were not Mexican Indians." Each spring from 1869 until 1871, Indians had stolen hundreds of horses from ranchers in the settlement, including stallions, mares, colts, and mules from the Marnoch ranch that Gabriel estimated were valued at well over five thousand dollars. He'd gone into Mexico to look for his stock after the 1871 raid, in which Indians had killed the wife of his neighbor Jesús Martinez and kidnapped brothers Clint and Jeff Smith on the nearby Cibolo.

Gabriel's Kickapoo friend, whom he'd befriended during the war, accompanied him to the various Indian camps—Kickapoo, Lipan, and Seminole—in Nacimiento, Coahuila. They found six horses at one of the Kickapoo camps. The Indians told Gabriel that "they had been captured in a fight that they had had with Comanches," and that he was "welcome to them." He brought them home.

In the same deposition, Marnoch mentioned correspondence he'd received at the time from officials at the Comanche reservation at Fort Sill, Oklahoma, who told him that his entire herd had been found on the reservation, taken by the soldiers, and sold. He never recovered the horses or received payment from the government.

Besides the Indian troubles, which were bad enough, the cotton embezzlement case had not reached a conclusion after five years, although it was finally settled in Marnoch's favor on June 7, 1872, when it was dismissed and the court ordered the plaintiffs to pay the defendant all the costs incurred. Despite this future positive development, Gabriel also had ongoing tax problems related to his father's estate and had been indicted for "the offence of taking up and using an estray horse without complying with the law regulating estrays." Marnoch had discovered a stray horse on his property and for an unknown reason neglected to follow the procedures necessary to locate the owner of the horse, beginning with reporting the presence of the stray to the local justice of the peace who was responsible for locating the owner.

Marnoch had failed to appear in court on November 13, 1871, to answer to the charge—again for an unknown reason—and a warrant was issued for his arrest.

When he was out in the field, he could forget about his troubles.

Helotes Creek, which ran for several miles through the Marnoch ranch, was spring and rain fed, varying in width from five to twenty-five feet, averaging several feet in depth depending on the season. Isolated pools formed along the creek bed in the dry summer months. On this late fall day, the creek was swollen after a rain, a good time to search for critters dislodged from their habitats.

Gabriel laid his bag and other field equipment at the bank of the creek. He walked to its edge and crouched on his haunches. He watched and listened but heard only the rustle of foliage as gusts of crisp wind blew from the north. In the spring and summer, he'd heard a cricket-like chirp and followed the notes to the muddy banks of the creek but could not find the creature that had made the sound. He was sure it was a frog of some type.

He moved closer to the edge and gently poked at the flora. He spied a salamander, light yellow, with brown chromatophores on its back and sides, giving it a mottled appearance. He got up to open his satchel and retrieved a jar. As he did so, he heard the unmistakable sound of horses' hooves. He grabbed his rifle.

In a few minutes, a man on horseback leading a saddled sorrel mare appeared on the path along the creek. The man stopped when he saw Marnoch. He jumped off his mount, pulling his rifle from its leather scabbard.

Gabriel eyed the man warily.

"Mr. Marnoch, I have a warrant for your arrest." He removed a piece of paper from his pocket and waved it.

Gabriel set his rifle down. He motioned for the constable to come toward him. The officer moved forward, close enough so that Marnoch could take the warrant. Gabriel looked at the legal document, and then in a swift motion, tore it into several pieces. He tossed the remnants into the creek. "No Meskin's gonna take me to jail," he spat.

Who overcomes by force hath overcome but half his foe.

—JOHN MILTON

3

Overcomes by Force

NOVEMBER 1871

Cesario Menchaca's gray eyes narrowed as he watched the remnants of the warrant float down the creek. He'd not been thrilled about having to arrest Gabriel Marnoch, an odd man who spent hours exploring caves and wading in the creek collecting frogs, snakes, lizards, and other creatures, and who was known to have a quick temper.

Un hombre extraño, muy curioso, and *un hombre loco* were a few observations uttered when Marnoch was mentioned. Even the Germans wondered about his specimen collecting. He kept hundreds of small reptiles and amphibians in jars of alcohol displayed upon shelves in his dining room, a most unappetizing arrangement.

Marnoch had failed to appear in court to answer to the charge that he'd been using an estray horse contrary to the law, a cumbersome process that involved notifying authorities, advertising the stray animal for a length of time, and posting a bond for it. Menchaca, as constable in the precinct in which Marnoch lived, was charged with arresting him. In his one month in the position, Menchaca had done nothing more strenuous or dangerous than serve a road report to some reviewers, for which he received a fee of four dollars.

He looked back at Marnoch, who glared at him with a smirk that amplified the constable's rage. At five feet eight, Menchaca was several inches shorter than Marnoch and seven years his senior, but he had the lean, hard body of a cowboy and was stronger than the Scotsman.

Menchaca strode to his horse and retrieved his rope. He turned around, shook out the noose, spun it in the air and lassoed the astonished scientist. He tightened the noose so that Marnoch's arms were pinned to his sides. The constable yanked Marnoch's arms together in front and handcuffed him.

Marnoch, shocked into speechlessness at being lassoed, finally found his voice. He demanded to be released. When Menchaca instead pulled him toward the mare, the scientist shouted curses at him. The curses turned to threats as Menchaca removed the rope and ordered him to mount the horse. Instead, Marnoch lifted his handcuffed hands, hit the horse's rump and yelled. She reared and ran off.

The constable saw the triumphant grin on Marnoch's face. In a swift motion, he looped the rope around Marnoch's body, and then mounted his horse, tying the end of the rope to the saddle horn. He gave a slight kick. As the horse trotted up the muddy bank, the rope grew taut. Marnoch sputtered and raged, tripping over rocks and tree roots as Menchaca led him through the settlement toward San Antonio, some twenty miles away.

Menchaca followed the path along Helotes Creek to its intersection with Bandera Road, his prisoner's curses and threats making him reconsider his new line of work. Since the end of the Civil War, the justice system in Texas had been in upheaval as one provisional government after another attempted to establish itself. Because of the erratic leadership and the new Texas Constitution of 1869, many law enforcement positions, including that of constable, which had been elected posts, became appointed jobs. Few wanted such positions under the Reconstruction government, which was fomenting so much violence and discord in the state.

Justice Anton Gugger had persuaded Menchaca to accept the position of constable of the Helotes precinct, knowing that he could handle a gun. In fact, Menchaca was a sharpshooter, a skill perhaps inherited from his father and grandfather, who'd both served as presidio soldiers under Spanish rule in Santa Rosa, Coahuila. Menchaca knew little about his parents, who'd both died by the time he was four, but he'd been told that his father, a red-headed *criollo* born in Santa Rosa, had been a valiant soldier for the Crown, fighting Apaches and Comanches for ten years before Mexico shed Spanish rule in 1821.

Menchaca was reared by relatives in Santa Rosa, a Mexican village in a valley surrounded by the Sierra Madre Oriental Mountains, ninety miles southwest of the border town of Eagle Pass, Texas. Santa Rosa had been founded in the eighteenth century as a mission with a military garrison in which his father had served, and Menchaca was fourteen in 1845 when the name of the town was changed to Melchor Músquiz, in honor of a resident patriot who'd fought against Spanish rule and who'd briefly become president of Mexico.

In 1853, at age twenty-two, Menchaca became a father for the first time. His son's mother, Maria Guadalupe Elguezabal, had grown up with him in Santa Rosa. Guadalupe was the granddaughter of a high-ranking Spanish military officer who became the interim governor of Coahuila y Tejas in 1799, holding the office until his death in 1805. Despite her notable bloodlines, a marriage proposal was not forthcoming; nevertheless, she followed Menchaca to San Antonio.

Seven years later, on May 2, 1860, Menchaca married Isabela Rivas. He'd left Maria Guadalupe and their son Manuel in the care of his older half-brother Miguel Menchaca, a veteran of the Texas Revolution of 1836 who lived on a farm in the Helotes settlement. Isabela was a descendant of *Isleños*, early San Antonio settlers from the Canary Islands. She was the sister of Menchaca's good friend Francisco Rivas who'd introduced the couple. They had four children—Emelia, Victoria, Josefa, and Donaciano—and had been living on their Helotes farm a few years before Isabela died on September 14, 1870. Just twenty-seven, she was buried in San Antonio at San Fernando cemetery, not far from its namesake church where they had been married.

Despite their fractured relationship, Menchaca and Maria Guadalupe had kept on good terms. Ten months previous to his arrest of Marnoch, in February 1871, Menchaca had helped survey a 160-acre property in the settlement for her, property that would one day pass to their son.

Now, here he was, dragging a screaming man at the end of a rope. And not just any man. Despite his oddities, Marnoch was a prominent member of the community. That he might have deserved such treatment was irrelevant. The astonished expressions on the faces of fellow ranchers and farmers as Menchaca passed their homesteads pulling his unhappy prisoner along made Marnoch's status perfectly clear.

APRIL 1872

News of Marnoch's arrest spread throughout the Helotes settlement like a cut that festers into a cankerous sore. Tensions between Mexicans and Anglos that had reached a fever pitch during the Mexican War some twenty-five years before had never been resolved. However, in the Helotes settlement, where the families were self-segregated by large expanses of land and where many of the German and Anglo property owners, including Marnoch himself, employed Mexican farm and ranch hands, a degree of mutual cooperation had been the rule.

After Marnoch's arrest, sides were drawn. The Mexicans felt Marnoch got what he deserved. The Germans, Anglos, and other ethnic whites were angry about Menchaca's high-handedness. Marnoch was so incensed about the humiliating arrest that he allegedly "put a bounty out for Menchaca," an offer of $500 to anyone who'd kill him, an extravagant sum valued at $9,500 in today's currency.

Marnoch's failure to appear for his court date caused his bail bond to be revoked and he was put in jail for an unknown length of time.

His brother John and friend José Angel Torres had each contributed a three-hundred-dollar bond to assure that Marnoch would show up. The judge issued a writ requiring all three men to appear in court the first Monday in February, 1872, to give a good reason why the defendant had not appeared at his first court date; otherwise their money would be forfeited.

There is no record of them appearing during the February session; however, five months after his arrest, Marnoch appeared in a Bexar County District courtroom. On April 4, 1872, his lawyer filed a motion to "quash the indictment," which was denied. As the jury trial commenced, Marnoch pled not guilty to violating the estray law. After deliberations, the jury found him guilty and assessed him a fine of ninety dollars, plus costs, amounting to what one newspaper said was "about $300." The next day, Marnoch's attorney presented a motion for a new trial, but the request was overruled. The newspaper account said, "With that money [$300], he [Marnoch] might have purchased about a dozen first-class ponies and kept out of jail."

Menchaca's stint as constable of Precinct 2 in Bexar County ended a month later on May 27, 1872, when he "failed to qualify." What that meant is unknown since no reason was given in the record. There were a variety of ways a person could fail to qualify, among them incompetence, official misconduct, intoxication, and the inability to secure a bond. When Menchaca was first appointed to the position, he'd been able to post a five-hundred-dollar bond. Such bonds were necessary in the case of lawsuits. It is possible, and even likely, that he was denied bond because of the Marnoch fiasco and therefore was unable to qualify. It is also possible that Menchaca had no desire to continue on in the position, which had resulted in a bounty on his head.

After the Marnoch trial had played out, focus turned to "one of the most horrible massacres that has ever been perpetrated on the frontier." At the end of April 1872, a wagon train carrying military supplies from San Antonio to Fort Stockton was attacked by a large band of "Indians, Mexicans, and deserters from the Army" at a place called Howard's Well about 150 miles northwest of San Antonio. The US Cavalry arrived to find the charred and blackened corpses of nine teamsters. Eight women and children had also been wounded or killed. One woman who'd been taken by the Indians escaped. When she returned to San Antonio to recover from her ordeal, her story stoked horror and outrage. Her husband had been burned at the stake, her mother shot and scalped; her baby had been scalped, had its ears cut off, then had its "brains dashed out."

Such atrocities had occurred before. The previous year, Kiowa Chief Satanta and warrior Big Tree had gathered a war party of more than a hundred Indians from several tribes, set out from the Fort Sill reservation to Texas, and attacked the wagon train of freighting contractor Henry Warren, killing him and five teamsters. They cut out the tongue of a sixth man and hung him face down over a fire. By the time soldiers arrived, he was burned to a crisp. The bodies of the others were "horribly bloody, mutilated, [and] fly-covered."

The San Antonio papers in the summer of 1872 were filled with stories of Indian fights, thefts, and killings, and of the federal government's ineffectual response. Rumors circulated that Satanta and Big Tree would be released from prison "in return for peace." Even after the Texas Legislature passed a resolution that "under no conditions whatever would the two Indians ever be freed," Texans, always wary of government promises, didn't believe them, a prescient stance considering that Texas Governor E. J. Davis paroled them both a year later. A widow who lived on the frontier sent a letter to the *San Antonio Daily Express* that was published August 28, 1872, summing up the state of affairs: "When I formerly took your paper, I was rich in cattle, sheep, and goatherds; now I am poor, having lost all my property, which would not be the case if the government of the country would give the people that protection which they were in the habit of receiving in the good old times of the past."

As raids on the frontier intensified, the Texas Legislature authorized twenty-four Minute Companies. These county detachments, called Minute Men troops, were composed of twenty men who would meet for ten days a month when the Indians were most active. "Considered Rangers, the Minute Men furnished everything except their arms, ammunition, and accouterments, which were supplied by the state and which remained state property," according to Frederick Wilkins, author of *The Law Comes to Texas: The Texas Rangers, 1870–1901*. When the call came to organize such a troop in neighboring Medina County, no shortage of men answered.

John Green and Cesario Menchaca were among them.

I do solemnly swear that I will bear true allegiance to the State of Texas, and that I will serve her honestly and faithfully against all her enemies or opposers whatsoever, and observe and obey the orders of the governor of the State, and the orders of the officers appointed over me.

—TEXAS RANGER OATH

4

Do Solemnly Swear

SEPTEMBER 1872

A crowd of citizens gathered on the balmy Sunday afternoon of September 1, 1872, in front of the new limestone Kendall County Courthouse in Boerne, Texas, to witness the induction of Minute Men Troop V of Medina County. The new company would be stationed at Castroville, thirty miles east of Boerne, protecting the town's western border, and the townspeople's enthusiasm was evident in their cheers of approval as the troop assembled. The festive atmosphere belied the danger that lay ahead for the Rangers.

The sun brought perspiration to the brow of Lieutenant George Haby as he viewed his men, mounted on their horses and lined up in front of him. Some of the horses shuffled and nickered, shaking their heads against the flies assaulting their eyes. Haby held up his right hand, and his men followed suit. They first tightened their reins to control the horses, and then raised their right hands, palms forward. The crowd quieted down as Haby administered and the men repeated their oath of office, ending with the time-honored phrase, "So help me God."

Sworn in, the men dismounted and stood in line to sign their enlistment papers and accept a few state-issued supplies: a Winchester carbine, cartridges, and a sling and swivel for their rifles. They were to supply everything else they'd need, including their own horse, a six-shooter, food, water, and blankets.

Haby, behind a long wooden table set up in the courtyard, observed his men, reasonably confident he'd accepted the best for the job. When news of his commission had gotten out, he'd been inundated with enlistment requests from angry settlers from his own county of Medina and from northwest Bexar. Their anger was justifiable, but it had to be controlled for the men to be effective in a Ranger unit.

Known as one of the "fighting Habys," Lieutenant Haby and his large extended family from Alsace, France, had been battling Indians since they put down stakes on the banks of the Medina River in 1848. An old Indian trail ran through their land and many encounters with natives ensued over the years. In 1870, as livestock thefts escalated, Lieutenant Haby's brother Nicolaus had killed an Indian he'd caught trying to steal his horses, leaving the corpse for the hogs to eat, an act of utter disdain that likely infuriated the already impassioned Indians. However, according to Nicolaus, who related the story years later, this event marked the last raid into the Haby Settlement.

At forty-two, Lieutenant Haby had no illusions about Ranger service, which primarily attracted young, single men looking for adventure, a fact borne out by the fifteen single men in his newly formed troop that included his nephew Leopold. A family man with a wife and seven children, the lieutenant was a farmer and stock raiser who also ran a grocery store and saloon. When approached to lead the Ranger troop, he must have hesitated. Ultimately, however, he accepted the commission.

The troop would gather only ten days a month—a few days before, during, and after the full moon when the Indians were most active—leaving him time to tend to family and personal business. The salary of twenty dollars a month was not a motivation since, because of its depleted treasury, the state's payroll promises were unlikely to be kept. Probably, like so many other stalwart Texans, he'd tired of the ineffectual response to local problems of a faraway government.

The lieutenant's officers—John Green, Adolph Wurzbach, Julius Heuchling, and James Van Riper—joined Haby behind the table to assist in mustering in the troops. The officers had all seen military service, and all were experienced Indian fighters. Green had been shot in the arm on one of his last forays against Indian marauders, but was fully recovered and ready for action. Second in command as first sergeant, he was level-headed, a trait necessary when leading a group of spirited, independent-minded men. Wurzbach, his second sergeant, had served in the Confederate forces, albeit reluctantly, as had so many from the county who'd been against secession.

Heuchling, his second corporal, had been in Captain Richarz's Frontier Force stationed at Ft. Inge near Uvalde. Because of the cash-strapped state treasury, the troop had been mustered out the year before, but not before killing several Kiowas and Comanches, including a chief who'd taunted them with a tomahawk upon which hung the scalps of four white women. Several of Haby's men had been in Richarz's company, and he was fortunate to have them. Van Riper, commissioned as first corporal, had served in the 21st Texas Cavalry during the Civil War. The commander of his regiment had written on the bottom of his discharge papers, "In every engagement with the enemy, he was always in the front rank."

Haby, more aware than ever of his stature, "short [and] stout," amidst his troop of mostly tall, lanky men, looked up to greet Frank Bihl, a strapping Medina county ranch hand. The lieutenant noted Bihl's lack of regard for the pretty girls batting their eyes at him at the courthouse plaza. Rumor had it that Bihl was in love with a married woman, a situation fraught with danger. Facing the dangers of military service was preferable to coming toe to toe with a betrayed husband. Haby hoped the young private would forget about the woman during his time away.

Joseph Burell took two carbines, signing for his half-brother, who was absent. Burell, in his early forties and married to the lieutenant's cousin, had been a Ranger during the Mexican war. Afterward, he traveled to California and stayed for five years. On his return in 1855, Burell learned that his mother had died and his father had remarried. His father thought he'd died and had named the son born to his new wife Joseph Michael. To avoid confusion, the elder went by Joseph, the younger, Mike. Despite the age difference and circumstances, the brothers were close.

All the men had some level of Indian-fighting experience and had adequate mounts. To the best of Haby's knowledge, they were men of good character—hard-working farmers, ranchers, or freighters. There were drinkers and gamblers among them, and perhaps a Lothario or two, but all knew what was expected of them while on scout.

And their lives were now in Haby's hands.

OCTOBER 1872

The troop arrived at the Green homestead in small groups throughout the morning of Sunday, October 13, 1872, joshing each other while hitching their horses to the rail fence.

One of the men guffawed and nudged Mike Burell, "Hey there, Runaway, can ya give us some pointers on how to get away from a passel of Injuns? Heard you're the best at that business." Mike returned a sheepish grin.

During his service in Richarz's frontier force, Burell had been sent on a scout with a few other privates. When they were near Carrizo Springs, about forty-five miles from the Mexican border, they came upon sixty Indians who began pursuit. Burell's horse tripped, and with the Indians almost upon him, he managed to upright the horse and climb back on amid flying bullets and arrows, making a "hair breath escape" back to camp. He'd been called "Runaway Mike" ever since.

Cesario Menchaca, his brother-in-law Francisco Rivas, and their neighbor Jesús Zepeda, who at age twenty-three was one of the youngest in the troop, soon arrived. The Zepeda and Rivas families had been the first to settle in northwest Bexar County in the late 1840s and early 1850s, respectively, and had had many encounters with Indians. The men may have ridden in with Frank Bihl and a few others who lived on nearby Medina County ranches and farms. Whether the tension between Menchaca and Green that would characterize their relationship surfaced at this time is unknown; however, Menchaca's enlistment indicates a defiance against those who still bore a grudge against him for his handling of Marnoch's arrest and a disregard of the alleged bounty.

At dinner in midafternoon, their lighthearted banter gave way to a more serious tone when the men commiserated with Private Frank Monier about his brother's stock loss the previous month.

In mid-September, Indians had attacked Theo Monier's wagon train camped on the Medina River, twelve miles above San Antonio, taking seven mules, each worth $125. Monier owned a freighting business, which employed several men, including his brother Frank. What made the theft so aggravating was that two years before, Indians had stolen all of Theo's mules—the sixty it took to pull his six wagons. They'd never been recovered. Last month, Theo tracked the raiders for almost two days to no avail. By the time Troop V caught wind of the theft, the culprits were long gone. Since President Grant's "Peace Policy" was still in effect, the Minute company could not pursue them to their villages and so there was nothing to be done.

The settlers' disgust at this policy was noted in a letter published by a writer from Bandera County: "Under the above order the Indians can settle in our very midst, steal all the horses in the county, kill all the men, women and children whom they may come across, and retire to their villages. We dare not molest them, or can only do so at the risk of being outlawed by the government that should protect us."

Corporal James Van Riper, who'd arrived with his brother William and brother-in-law Taylor Jones, both privates in the troop, sat with his fellow officers apart from the others. He noticed three-year-old Willie Green, his eyes big with wonder, peering at the excited Rangers from behind his mother's skirts. Mrs. Green, with one-year-old Johnny on her hip, hovered over the men, bringing more food and drink as plates and glasses emptied. Johnny was the same age as Van Riper's own little boy, Charlie.

Van Riper was proud to be serving with John Green, a family man and an exemplary leader. Van Riper believed Green was a "better frontiersman" than Lieutenant Haby. When Haby hesitated about a plan of action, the first sergeant "went ahead and led the way," and the troop followed. Haby didn't seem to mind; in fact, he relied heavily on his second in command, a tacit acknowledgement of Green's extensive experience as an Indian fighter.

Though only twenty-nine and a farmer, James Van Riper was an astute observer of people, a trait learned early in life that would help propel him to the highest law enforcement position in San Antonio thirty years later—city marshal, equivalent to today's police chief. Born in Waterloo, New York, in 1843, he grew up the oldest son in a family of six sons, two daughters, a self-effacing mother, and a father with wanderlust and dreams of wealth. In 1849, Garry Van Riper took the entire family—including wife Matilda and four children under the age of seven—across the country to Bakersfield, California, and "with a partner opened up a mine in an attempt to wrest a golden fortune from a miserly Mother Earth."

His father returned to New York to close up his business affairs and while he was gone, his partner sold his share of the mine to another man who refused to acknowledge Van Riper as a partner. With no title to the mine, his father had no recourse, and therefore, no livelihood.

He turned his attention to Texas, where he'd heard land was cheap. With two new sons added to the family and a drove of fine "blooded horses," the family made the trek from California to Texas in 1858. James was fifteen.

The family settled on land along Salado Creek in northern Bexar County and started a ranch where they ran cattle and bred horses from the stock they'd brought from California. Two more children were added to the Garry Van Riper family. James remained at home until 1861 when he joined the Texas Cavalry, serving until the close of the war.

By 1870, he'd married Kate Jones, who'd been raised on a nearby ranch in the Coker Settlement, being part of the Coker clan on her mother's side. He acquired his own ranch and was intent on farming and raising stock when the Indian depredations intensified. The "nights of terrifying uncertainty" took a toll on his family life. When he heard a Minute Men troop was being raised, he jumped at the chance to join.

At four in the afternoon, and none too soon as far as the men were concerned, the troop left Sergeant Green's ranch. They were "especially anxious to start" as they'd received a communication "that a man by the name of Sheppard [who lived in Bandera] had been shot by Indians." Before leaving the Green homestead, they'd also received notice that stock from the Leon Valley ranch of Frank Huebner and the Helotes ranches of Jake Hoffmann, Phillip Ruempel, Gabe Marnoch, and Ed Rivas had been stolen during the night.

As they rode across the Culebra prairie to the west, they discovered that seventy-six of Green's horses, his entire herd, had also been taken. It didn't take long to find the trail of the raiders, who'd left the remains of several horses, arrows protruding from their carcasses, about four miles from the Green homestead. Within minutes, twenty horses kicked up a mighty dust and flew after the renegades, their riders hooting and hollering after hours of pent-up rage.

After the initial burst of energy, the troop slowed to a trot. Lieutenant Haby and Sergeant Green in the lead, Van Riper and the other officers riding flank, they stopped along the trail at springs and creeks to water their horses. Upon reaching Mescal Spring, a tributary of the Medina River, they discovered the half-eaten carcass of a horse, strips of flesh cut off, its musculature covered with flies. Shaking their heads and muttering at the loss of another good horse, the troop traveled northwest, passing the intersection of Mitchell's Crossing at the Medina River, Sergeant Green's old stomping ground. The troop found the remains of another horse a few miles up the trail, where the Indians had "had a feast."

Soon, long gray shadows canopied the countryside as the sun disappeared behind the hills. The moon, a few days from its fullest orb, rose like a beacon, shimmering a ghostlike beam along "the old Indian trail" leading to the Hondo and Verde Creeks. A couple of hours before daybreak, Lieutenant Haby ordered his men to "secure sleep and rest," though they were eager to push on, knowing they were not far behind their quarry.

At daybreak, the men returned to the trail. At the head of the Hondo, they surprised a small band of Indians coming over a hill with a large herd of horses. The startled parties froze and stared at each other for several seconds, during which time Corporal Van Riper examined their dress and saddles and concluded they were "either Kickapoo or Comanche."

Suddenly, all hell broke loose. The troop charged, and one of the Indians rode to the front of the herd, halted it, and jumped from his horse, escaping into the brush. He was followed by all but two of his fellow raiders, who attempted to escape by climbing up the mountain on horseback. Finding it too steep, they too jumped off and ran into the brush.

After the troop secured the herd, "100 head of horses and one mule," Lieutenant Haby sent a group in search of the raiders, but they "had made good their escape," likely in some of the caves and caverns so prevalent in the Hill Country terrain. Another group went in search of horses the Indians may have abandoned, but were again unsuccessful.

Nevertheless, they were justifiably pleased with the result of the expedition. As Helotes Justice of the Peace Anton Gugger wrote after their return, "They [the Indians] made no resistance and our boys, without firing a shot, captured 101 horses."

Left to themselves, things tend to go from bad to worse.
—GEORGE E. WOODBURY (1855–1930),
AMERICAN AUTHOR AND POET

5

From Bad to Worse

NOVEMBER 1872–APRIL 1873

Looking back, Lieutenant Haby could see a progression of escalating calamities leading to the tragedy that occurred under his watch. After the company's successful October scout, President Grant was reelected. His victory on November 5, 1872, against Horace Greeley, who had the majority support of Texans, angered the Rangers who were vehemently against the president's Indian policy. As one San Antonio editorialist put it, Grant's policy was "based upon a ridiculous appeal to the better instincts of a race whose instincts have always been toward treachery, theft and destruction, and whose tender mercies are cruelty. It assumes to transform these human tigers into bleating lambs, by substituting sweet-meats and moral suasion for the sword."

Subsequent expeditions in the next four months yielded the recapture of only four horses. The Muster and Payroll records of Company V Minute Men of Medina County give only a few general descriptions of the troop's monthly activities. For example, in a sworn affidavit, Lieutenant Haby, asserted that his "company performed ten days services during the month of December 1872, following the trail of Indians who were present in the county and of whose presence he received notice." In January and February 1873, the only deviation in the report was the capture of four horses from Indians, two each month.

While there are no records or diaries detailing the day-to-day activities of Company V, the troop likely patterned their days much like other Ranger units of the era, with the biggest difference being that since the Minute Men were on duty only the ten days a month that Indians were most active, they spent more time in the field and on their mounts trailing and tracking. In the classic memoir *Six Years With the Texas Rangers, 1875–1881*, Ranger James B. Gillett chronicled the start of a scout. After roll call, about half the troop was put in charge of the remuda of horses and mules, with a mounted guard. Those Rangers not on duty often played cards or pitched horseshoes. With permission, they could hunt or fish in the area, and they sometimes participated in horse racing.

However, at the "first light moon" Gillett's Ranger troop rode to the headwaters of the nearest river to camp, while the captain sent out two smaller details of Rangers to the north and south to hunt for Indian trails. Those at camp waited in obscurity and "readiness to take up an Indian trail at a moment's notice."

For the most part, when Lieutenant Haby's troop began its scout, the men had already received word of livestock thefts and the tracking began posthaste. However, there were periods of downtime during their ten days together and it was at these times that "bad feelings" between Sergeant Green and Private Menchaca surfaced. Green treated Menchaca gruffly. They exchanged pointed barbs. Other than that, the two men stayed clear of each other.

Then in early March, Haby's second corporal, Julius Heuchling, was thrown in the Castroville jail on the charge of assault with intent to murder not one but two citizens of the Alsatian town. Castroville, hometown of a majority of the men in the troop, was located on the Medina River about twenty miles west of Helotes in eastern Medina County. Founded by empresario Henri Castro in 1844, many of the first settlers were from the French province of Alsace, although Heuchling had emigrated from Germany.

The night of March 3, 1873, twenty-five-year-old Heuchling stumbled out of the local saloon and staggered along the narrow streets of the village—a town of quaint European-style homes with steep thatched roofs. Somewhere along the route he encountered Castroville farmer Charles Smith, got in a scuffle, and cut him in the face. Smith ran off and Heuchling continued on, encountering Joseph Koenig, a farmer in his early fifties who was returning home from church. After a salutation, the inebriated Heuchling took offense when Koenig "coughed and spit out." Heuchling sicced a dog on him, and the farmer fell against a pasture fence as the canine pounced on him in a barking fury. Heuchling shooed the dog away, but instead of helping Koenig off the fence, the young man stabbed him. Heuchling ran off when he heard people coming towards them. He was quickly apprehended and when he woke up the next morning in jail, he claimed no knowledge of what he'd done. "I was very drunk," he later said in a voluntary statement to the court. "I did not know until the next morning what I was in jail for."

The saving grace of the debacle was that neither Smith nor Koenig had died from the assaults. Nevertheless, Heuchling had violated the Ranger code—the requirement for sobriety, honesty, and good moral character—and had brought disgrace to the outfit. Haby expelled him from the troop. Heuchling was later found guilty of simple assault in the Smith case, and assault and battery in the Koenig case. He was also assessed a fine of one dollar in each case.

That March, while Haby's former corporal languished in jail, two substitutes joined the troop's ranks: August Wurzbach filled in for his half-brother Adolph for an unknown reason that perhaps had something to do with Heuchling's imprisonment, and the lieutenant's cousin, Jacob Haby, substituted for Private Menchaca, who was sick.

In April, the lieutenant received orders to take his company to Duval County to assist the State Police in the pursuit and arrest of a "band of thieves and murderers, numbering sixty, under the command of Antonio Alvarado and Alberto Garza." Garza, nicknamed *Caballo Blanco* or White Horse, was a bandit and cattle rustler known for driving stolen cattle into isolated areas, killing them, skinning them, and then taking the hides to Mexico to sell. He'd robbed and pillaged a store in Concepción, a small town in Duval County, which prompted the order for assistance. Unfortunately, the town was more than 150 miles south of Castroville, three counties away. By the time Troop V arrived, the Mexican bandits had sought refuge in Mexico. Demoralized and tired, the company returned home.

Not long afterward, Haby learned that Private Bihl had been summoned to court to answer to the charge of adultery. Apparently, if the charge was true, and Haby had no reason to believe otherwise, the young Ranger's time away with the troop had fueled rather than extinguished his passion for his married paramour. The lieutenant was sure things couldn't get any worse.

He was wrong.

JULY 1873

The July scout started out on its designated schedule, two days before the full moon was to appear on the tenth. Lieutenant Haby noted that his men were more agitated than usual when they arrived at Sergeant Green's homestead. Their horses snorted and pawed at the dusty earth, mimicking their riders' anger. Two days before, a band of Indians had massacred a family on their way to a Sunday visit with friends several miles north of the town of Bandera. The Indians killed the parents instantly and mortally wounded three of their four children. Their ten-year-old son jumped off their wagon and into the woods, escaping a sure death.

The Indians killed another man near Hondo Creek before making their way south within a few miles of San Antonio, where they stole horses from several ranches near Leon Creek. Kickapoos and their Mexican allies who'd plundered through the region for several years were the likely culprits.

Since the US government's diplomatic pressure upon Mexican officials to stop the thefts had not worked, the US Secretary of War had given tacit approval for Army Colonel Ranald Mackenzie to wage a surprise attack in Mexico on May 18, 1873. He led more than four hundred soldiers and a few civilians across the Rio Grande to attack three Kickapoo villages forty miles from the border in the state of Coahuila. The soldiers had set fire to all their lodges, killed nineteen Indians, and took forty women and children prisoner. They also recaptured sixty-five horses with Texas brands.

Mackenzie had violated Mexican sovereignty; nevertheless, his superiors, Secretary of War William Belknap and General Philip H. Sheridan, commended his actions. The Texas legislature gave him "the grateful thanks of the people of our State" and the Mexican government, perhaps understanding its complicity, "dropped the matter."

Nevertheless, Mackenzie's action was akin to poking a stick into a beehive, and for the next several months, Indian raids and killings intensified. During the week of Troop V's July scout, "information had been received from all parts of the West that Indians were robbing and murdering with even more than usual activity."

The Rangers were eager to rid the country of the raiders once and for all. Their zeal may have been fueled by the knowledge that their company was slated to disband the next month. Instead of greeting each other with good-natured insults as they usually did at the beginning of a scout, the men dismounted and quickly assembled. Soon they were back on their saddles, following Sergeant Green in pursuit of the Indian trail through the northwest Bexar County ranches of

Tom Odom, Henry Bruhn, and Placido Herrera, where several horses had been stolen or killed.

The troop returned to Green's ranch in the evening after losing the trail. They made camp on a hill among stands of oaks half a mile south of the sergeant's homestead. Though no one said anything, the men knew that Green's wife was near childbirth, which was perhaps why he'd chosen to camp so near his home. He put Private Menchaca on guard duty.

The next morning as the men broke camp and saddled their horses, a shot rang out. Lieutenant Haby ran through the campsite toward the sound of the gunshot, and he saw Sergeant Green fall to the ground. In front of the prone sergeant was Private Menchaca, holding his Winchester carbine, an expression of stunned disbelief on his face. Private Zepeda ran toward Menchaca, asking him to put down his gun. Instead, Menchaca ran into the brush, turning just long enough to take a shot at Zepeda. Menchaca, probably the best shot in the company, had missed Zepeda on purpose.

After the initial shock, the troop flew into action. Haby sent one of his men to notify Justice of the Peace Anton Gugger; he sent another, probably Corporal Van Riper, to notify Green's wife. Leaving a couple of men to attend to his sergeant's corpse, he ordered the rest of the company to mount. They were going after the killer.

And so the Grand Jurors, aforesaid, upon their oath, aforesaid,
do say, that the said Cesario Menchaca, him the said John Green,
in the manner, by the means, at the time and place aforesaid feloniously,
willfully, and of his express malice aforethought did kill and murder . . .
—W. H. JACKSON, FOREMAN

6

Did Kill and Murder

JULY 1873

The posse rode through the thick brush as the sun rose from the east, promising another blistering midsummer day. With Menchaca on foot, Haby figured they'd be able to catch him with little trouble. The lieutenant, in fact, knew it was imperative to apprehend him as soon as possible, before he reached the labyrinth of caves that stretched underneath the hills. Tales of dogs chasing animals into the caves of Helotes and emerging on the other side of a mountain several miles from where they entered were staples of the settlement. The troop had chased bands of Indians who disappeared into the hills so completely that the Rangers wondered if they'd seen a mirage. If Menchaca got to one of the many entrances to the cave system, it would be impossible to find him.

Haby began to realize as morning turned to afternoon that Menchaca had made good his escape. How he'd managed to evade the fifteen or so riders who'd fanned out over several miles puzzled him.

Later, some in the troop told a newspaper reporter that it was possible the private was in "collusion" with the Indians, who'd helped him escape. Menchaca had grown up in Coahuila near several of the Kickapoo villages that Colonel Mackenzie had destroyed. Someone else in the troop told a reporter that Menchaca "was not sound in the head" and suggested he may have "committed suicide." But in the entire eleven months the troop had been together, the lieutenant had seen no evidence that Menchaca was crazy.

What became increasingly clear to Haby was that at least a few of the men were sympathetic to Menchaca's plight. While Sergeant Green apparently had problems with Menchaca, the private, who was genial and good-humored, was popular among the ranks. Was it possible that some of the Rangers had abetted his escape? The company's relentless pursuit of Menchaca over the next several days allayed Haby's suspicions even though their search was unsuccessful.

The inquest hearing, juried by six local ranchers—William Boerner, Frank Huebner, Charles Schuchardt, Phillip Ruempel, William Braun, and Friedrick Braun—revealed that Cesario Menchaca had shot Green with a gun "on the left side of the body" leaving a "mortal wound of the depth of twelve inches and of the breadth of half an inch," which instantly killed him. Upon this finding, a warrant was issued for Menchaca's arrest.

Six days after the shooting, on July 15, with Menchaca still at large, Lieutenant Haby was "suspended from duty." The Muster and Payroll Record for July 1873 does not indicate why he was suspended; however, there can be little doubt that Green's death and Menchaca's successful escape were the instigators. The record also indicates that new recruit Fred Specht was sworn in as first sergeant in place of Green, who was "killed July 14 [*sic*] by C. Manchaca [*sic*]," who "deserted July 14, 1873, with State Carbine." Jacob Haby, who'd once substituted for Menchaca, served the balance of the fugitive's term. Green had actually been shot and killed on July 9; it appears that Haby did not alert officials until several days later to give himself and his troop time to apprehend the fugitive.

The troop met again on the fifth of August, under the command of Sergeant Specht, and mustered out of service after their ten-day scout, on August 15, 1873.

Two weeks after Green's death, the following letter appeared in a San Antonio paper:

> *No man, who was ever slain upon this frontier, is more regretted than John Green. A German by birth, he was almost raised in this county [Bandera], and was well known in three or four adjacent counties, and none knew him but to admire him. Dear was he to the writer of this, who had known him for fifteen years. Simple and unpretending in his habits, he was one of the bravest and best Indian fighters on this frontier, and upon that account, we believe, he was murdered.*

OCTOBER 1873

In October, six Rangers from the troop received subpoenas from the District Court of Bexar County to give eyewitness testimony in the case to help secure an indictment for murder against Menchaca, who was still on the run. Of the six, at least one was likely less than enthusiastic upon receipt of his summons—Menchaca's brother-in-law Francisco Rivas. After his successful escape, Menchaca had returned to his 160-acre farm and hid in a cave on the property for several weeks. He apparently felt sufficiently safe from arrest to put his affairs in order—with his brother-in-law's help—before fleeing to Mexico. On August 20, 1873, with Rivas's assistance, he'd placed daughters Victoria, age ten, and Josefa, age five, in St. Joseph's Orphanage, and enrolled his eldest daughter Emelia, age twelve, at Ursuline Convent, both establishments in San Antonio. He left his eight-year-old son Donaciano in the care of his mother-in-law, also giving her guardianship over the four children.

Menchaca had taken up with a young woman from Castroville, Magdalena Forst, the daughter of Alsatian immigrants. No marriage record has been found for the couple; however, in many Mexican legal documents she is referred to as his wife. According to a Mexican affidavit, they had a son, José Pio, born in San Antonio on July 11, 1873, two days after the Green killing. Whether Menchaca was with Magdalena when she gave birth is unknown; however, he did arrange for her and their baby son to move to Mexico.

During the October District Court session, the testimony of Rivas, Fritz Braun (not to be confused with Friedrick Braun mentioned as participating in the inquest hearing), Charles Braun, Taylor Jones, Frank Bihl, and Jesús Zepeda helped to secure a murder indictment for Menchaca, issued October 15, 1873.

The legal document did little to appease the grieving Green family since, by then, it was common knowledge that Menchaca had successfully escaped to Mexico. Without money to entice a bounty hunter, there was little chance for the capture of a Mexican fugitive. There were countless stories of Mexicans who'd confessed to murders in Texas and escaped to Mexico only to be shielded by their government from extradition. In an 1874 case involving the murder of a family from Refugio County, the murderer was caught in Mexico and delivered back to the United States "not in accordance with the treaty [between Mexico and the United States], but upon the payment of a large reward, (or bribe,) paid in money by the relatives and friends" of the family.

Two years later, on October 13, 1875, the Bexar County District Attorney, likely pressed by Green's family and supporters, sent the 1873 murder indictment to Texas Governor Richard Coke, requesting that the state offer a reward for Menchaca's apprehension. Twelve days later, the governor authorized a two-hundred-dollar reward.

Two years later, with the reward offer having yielded no results, the Green family was incensed to learn that Menchaca was conducting legal affairs regarding his Helotes property from across the border.

Helotes farmer Francisco Sanchez had filed suit against Menchaca, alleging that he'd "abandoned his pre-emption right to public land on the ninth day of July 1873" after killing Texas Ranger John Green and fleeing to Mexico. Sanchez's affidavit of abandonment, dated January 28, 1877, alleged that he had worked the land on the Helotes for the previous three years and that it was rightfully his.

The suit mobilized Francisco Rivas, who'd taken over the legal affairs of his nieces and nephew after his mother's 1874 death, to file affidavits on their behalf. Rivas contacted Menchaca, who responded from Músquiz, Coahuila, Mexico, with his own legal document, transferring his 160 acres to his four children on June 22, 1877. On the children's behalf, Francisco filed for and received a patent for the land on March 15, 1878, based on the transfer document. Nevertheless, the case went to trial two years later. The Menchaca siblings won, and Sanchez was ordered to pay restitution and court costs.

In the summer of 1877, as the Menchaca land dispute played out, Green's family pressed Bexar County District Attorney M. G. Anderson to send a request to Governor Richard B. Hubbard to increase the two-hundred-dollar reward for Menchaca to five hundred dollars. They learned that Juan Coy, a former law enforcement officer who'd killed a Helotes resident in February 1877, had been apprehended "on the Rio Grande" and was in the Bexar County jail. The governor had authorized a five-hundred-dollar reward for Coy's capture, which led to a trial, conviction, and five years in the penitentiary. Perhaps an increase in the reward for Menchaca's capture from two hundred to five hundred dollars would incentivize his apprehension. On July 28, 1877, Anderson wrote a letter to the governor requesting an increased reward of five hundred dollars. Eleven days later, the family received their answer: "Due to our exhausted state of the appropriations this reward offer by my predecessor can not be increased."

The only sure thing about luck is that it will change.
—BRET HARTE (1836–1902), AMERICAN AUTHOR AND POET

7

Luck Will Change

DECEMBER 1873

While the Green and Menchaca families were struggling in the aftermath of John Green's killing, Gabriel Marnoch again found himself embroiled in legal problems. He'd been accused of the felony offense of "theft of a mare" in Kendall County and on December 10, 1873, retained four attorneys, two from Kendall County and two from Bexar County, to defend him, promising to pay three hundred dollars in silver coin as their fee. He and his sister Elizabeth were also involved as plaintiffs in another case involving the illegal seizure of livestock that belonged to Elizabeth. Justice Anton Gugger had ordered their seizure and sale for back taxes owed by the Marnoch siblings for their father's estate. The jury trial in that April 24, 1874, case vindicated the Marnochs, and Justice Gugger and Charles Braun, who'd purchased the livestock, were ordered to pay back the defendants for the stock. Gabriel was also found not guilty of theft of a mare in a Kendall County jury trial on April 8, 1875. However, he was unable to pay his lawyers' fees and they sued him.

In the summer of 1876, the Marnoch family lost title to their homestead and land when a judge ordered the property seized and sold in a public auction to the highest bidder so that the debt to their attorneys could be paid. Their lawyers gave the highest bid and took possession of the deeds. That same summer, Gabriel was charged with aggravated assault and battery. The record does not indicate whom he assaulted, but it is a safe bet that at least one of his attorneys was sporting a black eye. At a jury trial, Marnoch was found not guilty and released. Despite the altercation, the attorneys worked out a deal with Marnoch and his siblings, allowing them to continue to live in the family homestead while they worked out a way to purchase back the deeds.

SEPTEMBER 1877

Marnoch didn't let his legal woes get in the way of his work as a naturalist. He'd become a field correspondent for Professor Edward Drinker Cope, who was well known in the scientific circles of zoology and paleontology. He'd been a professor of zoology at Haverford College in Pennsylvania and had served as curator of herpetology at the Academy of Natural Sciences in Philadelphia. In 1870, he'd begun traveling the western United States acquiring fossils.

In the spring of 1877, Cope had written to Marnoch requesting his assistance "on an extended exploration" of Texas, an entreaty Marnoch was gratified to accept, even offering to finance and provide the "camp outfit"—food and other camping essentials.

The paleontologist visited San Antonio on September 17, 1877, with several prominent men of science, including entomologist Henry "Harry" Brous, to lecture on the geology of Texas and the importance of scientific study in the schools.

Marnoch attended the professor's lecture and then accompanied Cope and Brous back to his ranch. The men explored the Helotes creek and hills for three days before Brous decided to leave the group and return home. Cope stayed on. A few days later, the scientific exploration of fossil localities to the north of Helotes near Fort Concho began.

Cope's visit was the highlight of Gabriel's life as a naturalist. The professor, a neo-Lamarckian, was one of the leaders of the American School of evolution theorists who followed an abridged version of the theories of French scientist Jean-Baptiste Lamarck. These evolutionists believed in the "inheritance of acquired traits," a position contrasting with Darwin's theory of evolution by the natural selection of random variation.

Although at odds with Darwin's theory of the evolution of species, Cope was referenced in *The Descent of Man*, published in 1871. Darwin mentioned the professor's affirmation of a link between dinosaurs, reptiles, and birds, "the latter consisting of the ostrich-tribe . . . and of the Archaeopteryx, that strange Secondary bird having a long tail like that of a lizard."

Just prior to his Helotes trip, Professor Cope had purchased the scientific journal *The American Naturalist*, where his long-standing feud with fellow paleontologist Professor Othniel Marsh of Yale College had first been publicized four years before. The men, in a "bitter competition for priority of discovery and publication," had aired their differences over the years in the journal, which had a rapt audience of fellow scientists mesmerized by the dispute. Marsh's charges of errors, distortion, and fraud against Cope and the professor's countercharges were published in the spring and summer of 1873. The viciousness of Marsh's attacks and his resurrection of a mistake Cope had made in 1868 assembling a plesiosaur when "he placed the head on the end of the tail" had pushed Cope over the edge.

Gabriel Marnoch, who knew the sting of humiliation, likely appreciated Cope's purchase of the journal as an elegant response of vengeance against his foe.

The war between Marsh and Cope extended to the field, where they'd both initiated spying and counter-spying. The professor must have felt relatively safe from Marsh's emissaries in the "practically virgin fields" of Texas, since he made no objection to the two men who joined him and his host on the trip: Gabriel's brother George and "a Mexican named Pedro."

His concern was focused on the provisions, free though they were. Cope jotted in his diary that his host had presented him with a "miserable black horse," upon which was a "saddle . . . very dilapidated in appearance." The horses Gabriel hitched to the wagon were no better than "mere 'crow baits,'" and the professor saw that several hundred horses grazing in Marnoch's parched pasture were equally wretched. A prolonged drought that had begun in the early seventies likely had contributed to their poor condition.

When they stopped to camp the first night, Gabriel discovered he'd left their food, plates, utensils, and other important camping gear "lying on a table in his house." Perhaps the worst omission was the coffee mill. Although Cope was stunned at this oversight, Gabriel took it in stride. There was plenty of game and they had rifles.

As the two-week trip progressed through the hilly regions of forests, cliffs, and streams, Gabriel enjoyed himself immensely, while Dr. Cope was discomfited by Marnoch's driving. The wagon ventured off the road on occasion, ran over a few huge stones, and "pulled down a stone wall with the wheel." The professor was aghast when he saw Gabriel drive down a hill at full speed and "pitched out head first." Marnoch, sporting a few bloody abrasions, simply jumped back into the wagon and resumed the journey.

Despite his reckless driving, Marnoch and his party traveled at too slow a pace for the professor. When they reached the south branch of the Guadalupe River, Cope left them. Several days later, Gabriel, George, and Pedro caught up with him.

Their prolonged excursion into central Texas did not result in the discovery of "fossiliferous strata," which is what Cope was looking for. Gabriel was disappointed, but the scientist told him that "from a zoological point of view," the trip had been interesting and profitable.

They'd run into "wild beasts large and small," and Cope was able to obtain skins and skeletons from nearly all of them. He was most proud of a "fine [peccary]" he'd killed and skinned.

Gabriel basked in the aftermath of the expedition, which reinvigorated his enthusiasm for his own fieldwork in Helotes.

That spring of 1878, he finally discovered the source of the chirping he'd heard over the years. A little frog in a crevice of the cliff along the creek was the culprit. Less than an inch in length, it had mottled green skin, a large head, and small toe pads. He'd been drawn to it by its nocturnal call of chirps and short trills. In fact, it sounded like a cricket and was quite noisy for so small a creature.

He sent the specimen to Professor Cope, who'd declared the little frog a "new genus of Cystignathididoe" and gave it the scientific name *Syrrhophus marnockii* in honor of his field correspondent. At about the same time, Marnoch sold 320 acres of the family ranch to a man named John Baker for one thousand dollars and paid his lawyers five hundred from the sale. On February 11, 1878, they released the deed back to him and his siblings. Gabriel Marnoch had just one month to enjoy this turn of good luck.

MARCH 1878

The morning of March 18, 1878, started out innocuously enough. John Baker had requested that Marnoch accompany the survey party he'd enlisted to settle a dispute regarding the boundaries of the property Marnoch had sold him, which was adjacent to the ranch of Helotes postmaster Carl "Charles" Mueller. Baker and Mueller decided to settle the boundaries by a resurvey. The group included surveyor Luciano Navarro, Mueller, Mueller's brother John, Helotes ranchers William Boerner and Fred Biering, and a few others.

The party met at Biering's house for a meal before the survey. Mueller and his brother John had a jug of whiskey, from which they and Navarro liberally drank as the meal progressed.

Intoxicated, Mueller confronted Marnoch over an issue that had been simmering for quite some time. Marnoch, who wrote many letters and also mailed large boxes of specimens to scientific institutions around the country, had been a frequent customer of the Helotes Post Office, where he also received much correspondence. In the spring of 1877, he received correspondence from Professor Leidy, indicating that one of Marnoch's packages to him, which contained "turtle remains," had arrived in a state of "ruins." Marnoch had confronted the postmaster about this mishandled package, demanding recompense, which elicited bad feelings on both sides.

Not long after, Mueller received notice from Washington "charging him with official misconduct as postmaster," and he believed Marnoch had made the complaint.

The inebriated postmaster yelled across the table at Gabriel, "I know you've been writing to the post office department at Washington about me."

"You're a liar," Marnoch retorted.

Both Mueller brothers popped out of their chairs, fists in the air. Allegations and objections crescendoed until the entire survey party spilled outside Biering's homestead. Everyone quieted down for a while, and then Mueller "recommenced abusing . . . Marnoch very badly and threatening to whip him." Other members of the party stepped between them and "very soon [Marnoch] walked away, and returned after a short while with a shotgun."

The Muellers were livid. Both men, who were stouter than Marnoch, told him to put the gun down and "they would fight him." He refused. They "advanced upon him" and he retreated about twenty feet "holding his gun in front of him and telling them to stand back."

Charles stepped toward Marnoch with his right arm raised, and Gabriel told him again to "stand back." Instead, Charles tried to grab the muzzle of the gun and it went off, killing the postmaster. Marnoch silently put his gun down and waited for the law. He did not resist arrest.

Marnoch, who spent time in jail before a five-thousand-dollar bail bond was posted, was indicted for the murder of Charles Mueller on April 4, 1878. At his first trial in November of that year, the jury could not agree on a verdict and a mistrial was declared. At his second trial on May 17, 1879, the jury convicted him of murder in the second degree and sentenced him to confinement in the penitentiary for twenty years.

Marnoch's attorneys kept him out of prison while they appealed his murder conviction, and the appeals court remanded his case back to the district court for a new trial. The judge believed that the jurors weren't given appropriate directions regarding self-defense. Marnoch would never go back to trial. His lawyers were able to get continuances due to their inability to recall several important witnesses who'd moved out of the county. The murder case was finally dismissed in 1887.

Marnoch lived for nine years under the dark cloud of legal troubles due to the postmaster's killing. During that time, perhaps he pondered why the courtroom spectators cheered and clapped upon hearing the verdict when he was convicted of the postmaster's murder. Or perhaps he knew that their approval of his conviction was not simply about justice for the postmaster, but also for John Green.

PART TWO
1892–1903

*The desire to satisfy hunger, or any passion, such as vengeance,
is in its nature temporary, and can for a time be fully satisfied.*
—CHARLES DARWIN, THE DESCENT OF MAN

Where ignorance is bliss, 'tis folly to be wise.

—*Thomas Gray*

8

Ignorance Is Bliss

MARCH 1900

Deputy Sheriff Will Green and his counterpart from Las Cruces, New Mexico, Ben Williams, strode down Zavalla Street near downtown San Antonio in the early morning hours of March 20, 1900. The few people they passed noticed stern expressions under thick Kaiser mustaches. Their wide-brimmed felt hats covered dark, short-trimmed hair. What passersby didn't see were brass deputy badges on vests worn under knee-length jackets of broadcloth and holstered pistols slung low on their hips. Both lawmen felt the familiar rush of adrenaline in anticipation of the coming arrest, Williams perhaps more than Green, since the men they were after had eluded him for more than a month.

Deputy Williams had been on the trail of the fugitives, William "Billy" Wilson and Oscar Wilbur, since they had robbed the George D. Bowman & Son Bank of Las Cruces on February 12, taking $1,100. He'd traced them to San Antonio to a house recently purchased by Wilbur near two railroad tracks.

The evening before, when Chief Deputy James Van Riper had asked Green to assist Williams on the arrest, he'd been eager to oblige. At age thirty, Green had been a peace officer for eight years, and he preferred working with lawmen like the Las Cruces deputy who had a reputation as a "tough fighter and a good shot." Williams had been deputy to Pat Garrett, the famed sheriff of Doña Ana County, New Mexico, who killed Billy the Kid, the notorious outlaw and murderer.

The deputies arrived at the wood-frame bungalow near the corner of Zavalla and Medina Streets as the 6:50 train whistle blew. Green gazed up and down the residential street just a few blocks from the county jail, watching for Deputy Caruthers, who'd stayed at the station waiting for the judge to sign the arrest warrant.

Suddenly, the door to 916 Zavalla opened and two men emerged from the house. Dressed as "typical Western cowboys," they wore vests over linen shirts, neckerchiefs, denims, wide-brimmed hats, and boots. Holsters wrapped around their hips held pistols.

The cowboys sauntered onto the dusty street. Green raised an eyebrow at Williams as they made their way toward the men. The deputies passed the cowboys, Williams nodded, and he and Green turned around.

Deputy Williams called out, "Wilson, you and Wilbur are under arrest."

The cowboys spun around, reaching for their guns.

Wilson stopped short, his hand grazing his pistol handle, when he saw Deputy Williams's gun aimed at his heart.

Green drew a fraction faster than his opponent, Oscar Wilbur; nevertheless, the fugitive gripped his pistol, pointing at the deputy. They stared at each other in a standoff, which lasted a tense few seconds. Finally, Wilbur slowly put his gun down, and both bank robbers surrendered their weapons, just as Deputy Caruthers arrived with the warrant.

The next day, Deputy Sheriff Ben Williams and the two prisoners left on the Southern Pacific railroad train for Las Cruces. Green kept tabs on the trial. Wilbur and Wilson pled guilty and implicated two others from Las Cruces who they said had furnished the horses for their escape. After a four-day trial a month later, Wilson was given a ten-year sentence for bank robbery and Wilbur received a reduced sentence of five years. The accomplices were found not guilty. Six months later, New Mexico Governor Miguel Antonio Otero granted Wilbur, who'd testified for the territory, a full pardon.

The justice system worked in ways that seemed unfair—an admitted criminal turns state's evidence and is pardoned—yet Deputy Green had a stalwart belief in its efficacy. He'd joined law enforcement because he believed in justice, and perhaps for another, more compelling reason—to apprehend and bring to justice the man who'd killed his father. Cesario Menchaca was still a fugitive, twenty-seven years after the murder of John Green.

It is not clear when or how Will Green learned about the circumstances of his father's death; however, it appears that he had no knowledge of it while he was growing up and learned about it inadvertently, starting a chain of events that resurrected long-buried resentments and conflicts in his quest to bring Menchaca to justice.

July 1873

Will Green was just shy of four years old when his father died, his brother Johnny almost two. Will was old enough to recall the funeral attended by neighbors and his father's fellow Rangers held under the oak tree on the Green ranch. He did not know, however, that his father's burial site was at the spot where John Green had been killed. That he would learn later. His mother, nine months pregnant in widow's black, was heavy with child, and would give birth to daughter Mary just ten days after her husband's death. Some said Mary's birth was a blessing and that she'd help take away the sting of his father's loss. But if Will had had a choice between a squalling baby and his father, he wanted his father.

His mother didn't like to talk about John Green. Only twenty-four when her husband died, Augusta Specht Green was of the rugged pioneer stock whose Teutonic heritage had forged within her a reticence to rehash the past. With three small children to raise, she could ill afford to look back. All Will knew, either by design or omission, was that the Indians had killed his father. They were convenient culprits.

Soon, his father became a bittersweet memory kept in Will's heart and pulled out from time to time. What he learned about his father came from others—his uncles and his father's friends. The Van Ripers, James and William, who'd been in his father's troop, had told the young Will that John Green had been the best frontiersman around and that he was one of the bravest men they ever knew. Still, Will had memories of his father, filtered through his recollections of his mother.

Augusta had often been left alone with the children before John died. In addition to the ten-day scouts that were part of his Ranger duties, he frequently had to go into San Antonio to sell stock. Late one night when his father was gone, Will remembered barking dogs waking him. His mother had been antsy before he'd fallen asleep because Indians often came around during a full moon to steal horses, sometimes even shooting arrows through cabin windows and hitting the kerosene lanterns to start fires as a distraction while they took off with the stock.

That night, Will had watched Augusta grab her Winchester and carry it outside. He'd slipped out of bed and peeked through the door, which she'd left slightly ajar. The moon shone round and bright. Dark shadows stretched across the front lawn into the pasture where the horses were corralled inside a big rock fence that was a foot thick and several feet high. His mother walked gingerly, pointing the gun at a dark figure creeping along the top of the fence. She pulled the trigger.

Bang! Will jumped.

Plop! The dark figure fell to the ground on the other side of the fence.

Will's mother ran back to the cabin and bolted the door shut as Will scampered back to bed. He heard her pacing the floor, but soon the dogs quieted down and the night was still. He drifted off to sleep.

The next morning when Will's father returned, Augusta told him she might have shot an Indian and directed him to the corral.

When he came back to the house, he grinned. "You shot a big, black panther."

Augusta seemed surprised and maybe even relieved.

Will's mother had weathered the tragedy of losing her husband with the assistance of her brother-in-law Henry and her brother Adolph. They helped her tend the animals and plant the crops, and the cycle of farm and ranch life continued.

The Indian attacks also finally ended. The federal government—acknowledging that Grant's Peace Policy had failed to establish peace and in fact had caused a surge of Indian-White violence—gave approval for the army to take preemptive action against recalcitrant Indians. By 1875, with military harassment unrelenting and buffalo almost extinct, the Texas Indians returned to their reservations for good. Comanche leader Quanah Parker surrendered in June 1875, leading all of the "Comanche remnants" to the Fort Sill reservation.

On a more personal level, on February 5, 1878, five years after her husband's death, Augusta married Robert Robinson, an Irishman from Pennsylvania. Nine months later, Will had a new baby sister, Eleanora, and not long after that, his stepfather died. Just like that. There they were again, with another squalling baby and no father.

MARCH 1878

Six weeks after Augusta's wedding, Gabe Marnoch killed the town postmaster.

The killing roused a lot of anger. Will, who was nine, heard the word "lynching," over and over again, spit out by irate townsmen. Although at the time Will didn't know what the word meant, he knew it wasn't good. Marnoch, who'd been taken to jail in San Antonio, was lucky to be there, because there were many who were out for blood.

By the time of the postmaster's funeral, held on his ranch a few days after the murder and attended by most of the townspeople, word was out that Marnoch was saying that he had returned to the Mueller property with a gun "for the purpose of procuring zoological specimens, which he was in the habit of doing," and that he had a witness to prove it.

Even young Will knew that a breech-loading double-barreled shotgun would have blown a critter to bits, leaving nothing to examine. Marnoch or his lawyers eventually realized the outrageousness of his claim, because he settled on a plea of self-defense against Mueller. From what Will could figure out from the rumors around him, the postmaster was the one who picked the fight, but everybody blamed Marnoch for what happened.

Over the next few years, Marnoch spent a lot of time at the Bexar County Courthouse. After he was found guilty at his second trial, Marnoch had returned to his ranch on appeal, something that didn't set well with many of the townspeople, and most especially Augusta. Will's mother seemed to take Marnoch's freedom as a personal affront.

That's where things stood when Will's stepfather died. Mr. Robinson was buried next to Will's father on a little knoll under a big oak tree in the family cemetery, about a half-mile from the Green homestead. Two years after Mr. Robinson passed on, Augusta married again. Julius Ballscheit was barely off the boat from Germany when the couple wed on May 29, 1882. Will's new stepdad spoke only German and was a no-nonsense, hard-working farmer. He and Will's mother presented the family with a baby girl, Emmy, the summer of 1883, the last addition to the family. Will's new stepfather also had better luck staying alive. He and Augusta were married for forty-one years.

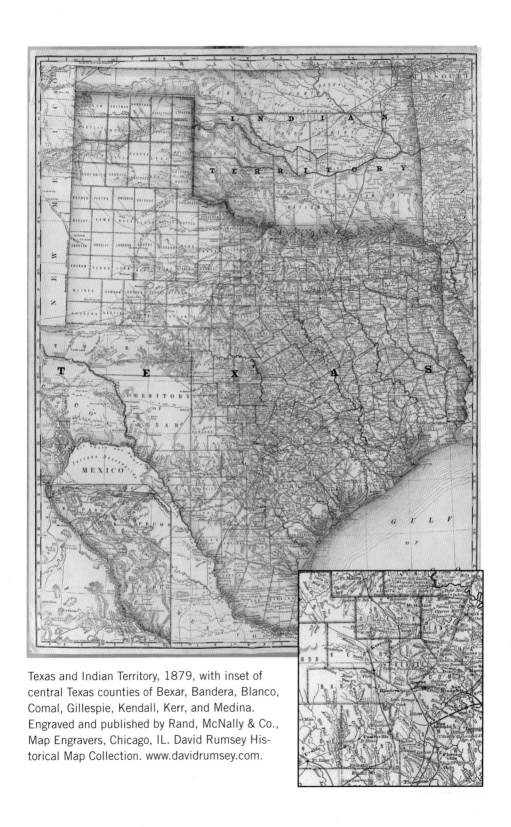

Texas and Indian Territory, 1879, with inset of
central Texas counties of Bexar, Bandera, Blanco,
Comal, Gillespie, Kendall, Kerr, and Medina.
Engraved and published by Rand, McNally & Co.,
Map Engravers, Chicago, IL. David Rumsey His-
torical Map Collection. www.davidrumsey.com.

Helotes rancher John F. Green, in this late-1860s photograph, was commissioned first sergeant of Minute Men Troop V of Medina County, a Texas Ranger troop. He served for almost a year until fellow ranger Private Cesario Menchaca shot and killed him on July 9, 1873, in a slaying steeped in mystery.

Green's widow Augusta (née Specht) married third husband Julius Ballscheit in 1882, and the couple is shown here in 1916 with their grandchildren. Augusta told her descendants that Indians killed her first husband.

COURTESY OF RUTH LAMPMAN

Frontier naturalist Gabriel W. Marnoch, correspondent and guide of noted paleontologist and herpetologist Edward Drinker Cope, discovered two amphibian and two reptile species in the limestone cliffs in the Helotes hills, including the Cliff Chirping Frog, *Eleutherodactylus (Syrrhophus) marnockii*. Marnoch's altercation with Menchaca is alleged to have played a role in Sgt. Green's death.

COURTESY OF CATHERINE MARNOCH VISTUBA

The Marnoch homestead, built in 1859, is the oldest residence in Helotes. The house, shown in this early 1900s photograph, was on a 1,515-acre ranch encompassing land that later became the town of Helotes. Dr. George Frederick Marnoch, an 1826 licentiate of the Royal College of Surgeons of Edinburgh, Scotland, immigrated with his family to Helotes in 1858.

COURTESY OF RODENNA BIERING

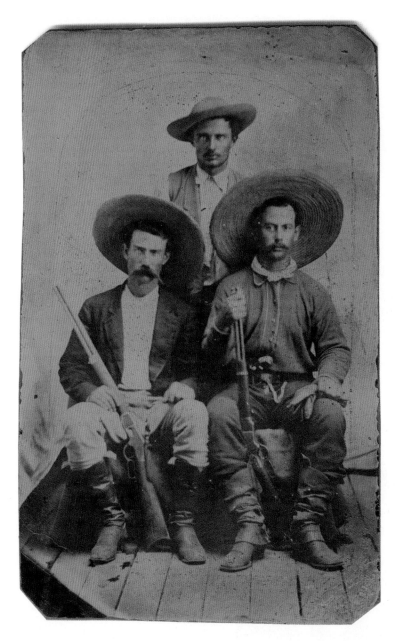

Rare tintype, circa 1872 or 1873, believed to be Jacob Haby, Joseph Beck, and Joseph Burell Jr., found in a tin box of important documents owned by Haby. Related by marriage, these men served in Minute Men Troop V of Medina County. Haby is holding an 1866 Model Winchester rifle and Burell is holding an 1866 Model Winchester Carbine, the type issued by the state to its ranging units.

COURTESY OF MR. & MRS. DONALD M. YENA COLLECTION

Police Capt. Will F. Green, July 29, 1927, holding a belt and scabbard taken from a notorious cattle thief in the "wild and wooly days." Green pursued Menchaca's extradition from Mexico after he learned that Menchaca killed his father. This photograph was taken a few months before Green became Chief of Detectives.

SAN ANTONIO LIGHT COLLECTION, 0867-D, UNIVERSITY OF TEXAS AT SAN ANTONIO LIBRARIES SPECIAL COLLECTION

Cesario Menchaca's son-in-law Lorenzo Morales was a leader in Helotes's Hispanic community, founding a Legal Aid Society in the late nineteenth century. He also served with Gabriel W. Marnoch as a trustee for the Los Reyes School. He bailed his father-in-law out of a Mexican jail after Menchaca's extradition hearing in 1903.

COURTESY OF LAWRENCE MORALES

Frank Bihl, with wife Mary Susan Eastwood Zimmerlie, and their family, circa 1892. A member of the Minute Men troop, Bihl assisted in Menchaca's escape after Menchaca shot Green.
COURTESY OF LORI BIHL DUNN

The San Antonio Police Department, circa 1901. Mounted Patrol Officer Will Green is in the top row, first person on the right. City Marshal James M. Van Riper, who served under Sergeant John Green as first corporal in Minute Men Troop V of Medina County, is seated in the first row, second person from the right.
COURTESY OF WILLIAM "BILL" GIBSON

Francisco Rivas, shown in this 1877 photograph with wife Ana Maria Garcia, was a member of the Minute Men troop and Cesario Menchaca's brother-in-law. Rivas became guardian of Menchaca's children after Menchaca fled to Mexico.
COURTESY OF CAROL SCHMIDT

Cesario Menchaca's daughter Victoria married Lorenzo Morales in 1883. She passed away five years later, leaving two children, Juanita and Lorenzo II. Many of their descendants still live in Helotes.
COURTESY OF LEANN EVANS HOLT

SPRING 1885

Like his father, Will preferred the open range and the company of
ponies. Although the demand for horses was waning because of the
advent of the railway and electric trolleys, farmers and ranchers still
needed good mounts for work and transportation. By the end of the
eighties, Will had become "famous as a breaker of wild horses."

Will could look at a pony and know its attributes. Some were suitable only as workhorses: large, beefy, and somewhat slow animals that
could pull a plow or heavy wagon. What most ranchmen were looking for, however, were good cow-ponies, intelligent and "small, patently
sound in body and quick of foot." If fast over long distances, they were
called "long horses," if fast in spurts, they could be "cutters," or if not shy
with a cowboy and lariat, "ropers." If a pony met all these qualifications,
it was regarded as an aristocrat and considered of "royal rank." If sold,
such well-trained cow-ponies were worth three times the normal rate.

During this time, Green and a partner drove a herd of horses to
Maine. Locals in the small town of Augusta heard that a real Texas
man who could "throw a lasso as lassos are thrown in the wild and
wooly west" was in their midst. They sent a "young man dressed in
fancy togs" to see if the rumor was true.

Green emerged from the livery stable where he and his riding
partner had headquartered and verified the rumor.

The young man said, "Suppose you put a rope on me?"

Green was game. He told the man to "make a running start."

At about thirty feet, the young man "found himself tied up in a
double bow-knot, with ropes around his arms, legs and head, and lying
comfortably on the ground."

The man was so impressed by the feat that he brought several of
his friends back to the stable to be lassoed by Green.

During his several-week stay, Will was amused to learn that the
locals referred to him as "Deacon Green," an appellation attributed to

what they considered his "pious appearance," perhaps in reference to his courteous manners and quiet demeanor.

His trip to Maine had been among the happiest in his life, his skill as a roper at its peak. He'd also astounded the northerners with "his fleetness of foot," a skill he used to great advantage later when pursuing criminals. "When Will Green takes after you, it ain't no use to go for your hat and leave, for you is bound to go down," was a familiar saying to those who'd tried to evade capture.

During the years Will worked as a horsebreaker, he followed with interest the careers of his father's friends James and William Van Riper, who were involved in just about every important criminal case in the county. As deputy sheriffs and deputy US marshals, the Van Riper brothers assisted in the dissolution of the Helotes Gang, outlaws who held up stages and robbed country stores, post offices, and churches throughout the region, but whose base of operation was in the hamlet of Leon Springs, just up the road from the Helotes settlement.

Related by marriage and by nefarious deeds, the gang began to unravel in 1885 when two of them shot and killed a deputy US marshal as he was escorting them on a train to San Antonio from Austin, where they'd been tried and convicted of robbing a post office. One of the killers got away and the Van Ripers were part of the posse that caught him the next day. Not long after, they also caught up with another gang member who'd escaped from prison. He refused to give himself up, so paid the ultimate price for his stubbornness.

Proving the old adage, "There's no honor among thieves," the gang unraveled even further as one by one, they began to squeal on each other. In the summer of 1886, James Van Riper and two fellow deputy US marshals found the skeleton of one of the gang members, Frank Harris, at the bottom of a cave in the Helotes hills. Harris had gone missing two years before. Fellow gang member Francis Scott was convicted of Harris's murder during the spring term of 1887, and was sentenced to life in the penitentiary.

With the majority of the criminals dead or in prison, the Helotes Gang collapsed, taking with it the tension in the settlement that had cracked in the air like an electrical storm in a drought that had lasted half a decade.

A month after the Scott trial, on July 2, 1887, the murder case against Marnoch was dismissed. With no more fanfare than a signature on a legal document, he was legally free. James Van Riper, who'd been one of the many deputies over the years charged with summoning witnesses for the case, explained that subpoenas could not be executed to vital witnesses, several of whom lived outside the county and at least one of whom had left the country. Marnoch's lawyers convinced the court that their client couldn't get a fair trial without them.

The decision to dismiss angered many of the townsfolk, but after so many years, passions had subsided and they resigned themselves to living in the same community with a "refugee from justice."

SEPTEMBER 1891

James and William Van Riper moved from their northwest Bexar County ranches to San Antonio in the early 1890s. Will, a frequent visitor to the brothers' homes, met and fell in love with Emelie Boubel Ackermann, a widow five years his senior, a resident of the Alamo City. Her husband, Andrew, a private in the US Army who'd served as a provost guard at Fort Leavenworth, Kansas, had died in 1887, leaving her with two small children.

Emelie was the fourth child and second daughter of Nicholas and Wilhelmina "Lena" Boubel. French by birth, Nicholas married German-born Lena Tatos in 1852 in New Orleans, moving to San Antonio the following year. As longtime residents of the city, the Boubels, who raised eight children, were well known and well regarded. When Will met his future father-in-law, Boubel, who'd worked as both a jeweler and stonemason, was engaged as a house painter. He later founded a soap manufacturing plant on Villita Street with his sons.

On Thursday evening, September 10, 1891, William Green, just shy of twenty-two years old, married twenty-seven-year-old Emelie at the Boubel homestead. County Judge Samuel W. McAllister presided at the "festive" affair. Will became stepfather to seven-year-old John and five-year-old Bertha. Five months later, on February 14, 1892, their first child, William Emil Green, was born.

That summer, on July 2, 1892, Will accompanied his mother, stepfather, and siblings to the Bexar County Courthouse. They refiled a claim on behalf of his deceased father against the United States Government and the Kickapoo tribe of Indians for the loss of 105 horses valued at $4,560, under the provisions of the new Indian Depredation Act of March 3, 1891, which had been enacted to compensate settlers who lost property to Indian tribes "in amity" with the United States. Congress had heeded the pleas of hundreds of stockmen on the frontier who'd lost horses and cattle during the chaotic years after the Civil War, vesting jurisdiction for losses caused by Indians in the US Court of Claims.

It is very likely during this time that Will learned the truth about his father's death, as his subsequent actions showed. During the deposition for the claim, his mother related the dates and circumstances of her late husband's stock losses. It is also likely, although not included in the deposition, that she acknowledged that the Indians who were responsible for their stock losses were not responsible for her husband's death. She likely mentioned this inadvertently while describing the various horse thefts. Even if Indians had killed John Green, the Indian Depredation Act and various court rulings had made it clear that personal suffering or injuries were not compensable depredation claims.

How Will felt upon learning the truth about his father's death is unknown; however, his actions afterward indicate an unrelenting desire for "justice." His brother Johnny, with righteous anger, confronted Menchaca's relatives whenever he came across them in the settlement. Will's temperament and years of observing the Van Ripers' law enforcement careers dictated another course.

He decided to run for constable in Bexar County's Precinct 2. A few months later, on November 8, 1892, Will Green was elected to the same post once held by his father's killer. His main duties were to summon witnesses and bring offenders to justice.

Revenge is a dish which is [best] served cold.
—SPANISH PROVERB

9

Revenge Best Served Cold

SUMMER 1893

In the summer of 1893, Constable Green rode through San Antonio's main plaza amid the clatter of carpenters and masons building a new county courthouse. Begun in the summer of 1891, the four-story building of native Texas granite and red sandstone would not be completed until late 1895. So, Will tied his horse in front of the three-story former Masonic building on the east side of Soledad Street that had served as the county courthouse since 1872, replacing the old "bat cave."

Green walked past two iron gates into the lobby, up the stairs to the second story District Court room and then into a passage leading to the district clerk's office, where he requested the paperwork from the *State of Texas vs. Cesario Menchaca* murder case.

A deputy district clerk returned from the vault with a large book. He placed the *Criminal Minutes for 1869–1873* on a desk and opened it, flipping pages until he found the notation for "October 15, 1873, *State of Texas versus Cesario Menchaca*, Case #783: Bill of Indictment for Murder." Nothing else was written in the minutes. The clerk returned to the vault as Will focused on the words on the page.

Several minutes later, the clerk returned with a judge's docket book for the most recent term, May 1893. Case #783 had been continued for twenty years and was the oldest case on the docket. Armed with the case number, the deputy clerk went back to the vault to locate the file associated with the case number.

After several minutes he returned, shaking his head. No file. He picked up a pencil and wrote on the docket book, "Last order – No papers," as a notation for the case.

Stunned, Will pressed the clerk for another look, upon which the clerk invited the constable into the vault for his own perusal. When another search turned up no indictment paperwork, Will thanked the clerk and left.

On the first floor, Will made his way to the county clerk's office and identified himself to one of the deputy clerks and requested the county commissioner's minute book for 1873.

Will paged through the thick ledger until he stumbled across a familiar name—Anton Gugger, who'd been justice of the peace in Precinct 2 when Will's father was killed. Gugger, who had died in 1881, had held an inquest and rented horses after John Green's murder, no doubt to use in pursuit of the killer. Underneath Gugger's name were the names of Constable Charles Braun, who had summoned the inquest jury, and the jury members: Frank Huebner, Charles Schuchardt, William Boerner, Phillip Ruempel, William Braun, and Friedrick Braun.

Will knew them all. Boerner was, in fact, county commissioner for Precinct 2.

Over the next several weeks, Will visited each of the men who'd been on the inquest jury. Their responses to his inquiries were all similar: *Yeah, Menchaca shot him. Not sure why. Heard he went to Mexico. Wish you luck. Probably best to leave it alone.*

His inquiries to Menchaca's relatives regarding his whereabouts in Mexico were similarly frustrating: *Quien sabe?* Who knows?

Rather than thwart his quest, the continued negative reaction galvanized Green. However, he was unable to advance the case. A constable had only so much authority, and Will, who would later be described as a "strict officer," was intent on proceeding on a legal course of action against Menchaca, which meant pursuing extradition, which he couldn't do without the official indictment, wherever it was.

Even with the paperwork, Will could not have chosen a worse time to attempt this legal action. An extradition trial in San Antonio in July 1892, for Carmen Ybañez, a Mexican citizen wanted for murders in Mexico committed during a revolutionist plot to overthrow the Porfirio Díaz regime, had ended with a denial of Mexico's request for extradition. Presiding Judge J. H. McLeary said, "If Ybañez is given up by the United States, he had better have his life insured before being placed in the hands of the Mexican authorities."

Although Ybañez was later sentenced to three years in a US penitentiary for violating US neutrality laws, the Mexican government was incensed that the United States would not deliver the murdering "revolutionist" to them. Under the circumstances, it was unlikely the Mexican government would agree to the extradition of one of its citizens indicted for a murder that had occurred some twenty years before.

Will bided his time, gaining experience in law enforcement with another run and win as constable in November 1894. He resigned eighteen months later and moved his family to the Alamo City where he worked as a deputy constable in Precinct 1 for a short stint. He then joined the Bexar County Sheriff's Department, serving as a deputy sheriff under Sheriff John P. Campbell, a former Texas Ranger, and James Van Riper, Campbell's chief deputy.

SUMMER 1895

In the early 1890s, San Antonio was the largest city in Texas with a population of nearly 38,000, more than triple its 1870 census count.

The growing town had "three main railroad lines, a 'perfect' system of water works, the purest water, wood block-paved plazas and streets, several electric street car systems, the prettiest Opera and Club House in the South, good electric lighting and gas systems . . . three daily newspapers, the most important military post in the US, and immense markets for horses, cattle, wool and cotton."

Just a few years before in a revival meeting in the Alamo City, the Reverend Dixie Williams, a famous evangelist of the era, had "roared that San Antonio was the wickedest city in the Union, not excluding Washington City which, he shouted, was the wickedest city out of hell." At that time, San Antonio had a large number of gambling houses and saloons where drunken brawls, murders, and illicit liaisons were the norm. Notorious gunslingers Ben Thompson and King Fisher were shot and killed at the Vaudeville Variety Theatre in 1884. A year earlier, "opium dens operated wide open on [South] Flores Street."

By the beginning of the nineties, however, the bawdy nightlife began to fade away, and Will saw opportunity in the burgeoning metropolis twenty miles from Helotes. In the summer of 1895, he moved his family, now including daughters Ida and Ellen, to a cottage near the homes of James and William Van Riper, in "one of the most charming" areas of San Antonio, a neighborhood with "fine residences" along and intersecting North Flores. Behind North Flores flowed an irrigation ditch, its banks "fringed with water plants, and embowered with trees and shrubbery." Footbridges spanned the five-foot-wide *acequia* giving occupants and visitors access to lush lawns, gardens, and "pretty cottages."

Not long after Will relocated to San Antonio, a second extradition trial for Carmen Ybañez resulted in another refusal to return him to Mexico. US authorities deemed his offense as "political," a charge not extraditable under the US–Mexico treaty. With Mexican authorities newly inflamed against the United States, Green continued to bide his time.

Two years later, in the spring of 1897, the criminal docket of the Thirty-seventh District Court had grown so large that Justice Robert B. Green ordered a special term of the court be instituted that summer. Justice Green (no relation to William Green), who'd served as district court judge for four years, was known as a "capable administrator" and no doubt felt that so many old cases lingering on his docket were a serious obstacle to efficiency, not to mention justice.

Five hundred cases were on the docket, "some of them . . . as far back as the seventies." A newspaper reporter wrote, "Among the number are about 50 murder cases, many of which are of long standing, the trials having been postponed from time [to] time in some instances, and in others the State has failed to get witnesses and the cases have dragged along."

News of the special session spurred Deputy William Green to action. He knew that the *State of Texas vs. Cesario Menchaca* case, now twenty-four years old, was the longest-standing indictment on the criminal docket. Justice Green would be loath to allow a continuance. Now was the time to do whatever was necessary to bring his father's killer to justice.

Man . . . cannot learn to forget, but hangs on the past:
however far or fast he runs, that chain runs with him.

—Friedrich Nietzsche

10

Chains of the Past

Spring 1897

Adjusting his eyes in the dim attic loft, Gabriel Marnoch, almost
sixty and balding, shuffled about amid trunks, old furniture, and his
overflow collection of mounted wildlife and jars of herpetological
specimens. His eyes rested on a jar containing a short-lined skink
like the one he'd sent to the Smithsonian in 1883, fourteen years ago.
He moved the jar over and placed another next to it. The attic was
cramped. Two stone chimneys set ten feet apart in the middle of the
attic interrupted the flow of the room. Because of the chimneys, the
sunlight coming through the small dormer windows on either end
was insufficient for viewing his specimens and he used a kerosene
lantern to brighten the room.

Marnoch had had to take over the space in the attic as his collection grew, despite various donations to institutions around the country. The primary collection of fossils and specimens was in the dining
room on the first floor, along with his library. His wife was not pleased
with the arrangement. Shelves of fossils and jars of snakes and reptiles
in alcohol, as well as "old books that gave the room a musty odor," were

not conducive to a hearty appetite. But the specimens had resided there long before his 1882 marriage to Carmel Treviño, and with so many mouths to feed—now four sons and three daughters—and money tight, perhaps a hearty appetite was something to be discouraged.

Marnoch walked past shelves of specimens. Near the four-paned dormer window facing north were small tables and stands devoted to his collection of mounted wildlife. He brushed past a stuffed panther and looked out the window at the Helotes Creek snaking through the family ranchland. His eyes rested on the limestone cliff where he'd made the discovery of the cliff frog that had solidified his standing in the scientific community and promised him immortality as a naturalist.

Since that time, in addition to his work with Cope, Marnoch had become a correspondent of Dr. Elliott Coues, a renowned American ornithologist, historian, and naturalist, to whom he'd sent a specimen of a solid-hoofed pig. He'd also corresponded with geologist Charles Abiathar White, to whom he sent cretaceous fossils. In his continued communication with Cope, Marnoch had sent what Cope considered an "important specimen"—a portion of a cranium of a sabre-tooth tiger Marnoch had found in south Texas. Throughout the 1880s, Marnoch collected and sent hundreds of specimens to the Smithsonian, among them the Texas banded gecko, western barking frog, cliff chirping frog, Texas alligator lizard, spot-tailed earless lizard, short-lined skink, chorus frog, spadefoot frog, Texas Rosebelly lizard, black-necked garter snake, and the smooth earth snake. He'd submitted his name to *The Naturalist's Directory* and the *International Scientists' Directory* under the listings Zoology, Herpetology, Palaeontology, Collection, and Exchange.

In addition to his interest in the natural sciences, Marnoch was also drawn to the agricultural sciences. In the spring of 1880, he planted an experimental Egyptian corn, Dhura, and harvested fifty to sixty bushels per acre that summer. He wrote in a report to the US Commissioner of Agriculture that "the ground seed makes good bread; corn should be good in arid regions."

By 1886, despite the murder conviction for the postmaster hanging over his head, Marnoch was also sought after for his expertise in the geological sciences. That year, he served as a guide to Robert T. Hill, then employed as an assistant paleontologist by the United States Geological Survey. Hill had traveled to the area to investigate fossil localities of the Cretaceous era. Marnoch took him to "an abrupt elevation" in the vicinity of the Helotes creek, an escarpment several miles wide that he'd also shown to Edward Drinker Cope upon his 1878 visit and who'd written about it in a scientific journal in 1880. Hill published an article about the discovery in 1887—the same year that Marnoch's murder indictment was dismissed—in the *American Journal of Science*. Hill, who gained prominence as a geologist after this article was published, described the fault zone, which became known as the Balcones Fault. In the Helotes region, the western part of the fault rose several hundred feet and was topped by wooded hills with large artesian wells and springs beneath. The area became known as the Edwards Plateau. On the eastern part of the fault were the beginnings of the Coastal Plains.

While Marnoch's legal problems ended and his scientific capital continued to rise, the once 1,515-acre ranch by 1889 had dwindled down to 450 acres, 290 of which were sold so that Gabriel could purchase his siblings' portions of the family homestead. The following year, his taxes were assessed for 160 acres, with livestock holdings of twenty-five horses and mules and twenty-five head of cattle. The value of his property was assessed at $640.

Marnoch perhaps thought his financial situation would improve when the new Indian Depredation Act of March 3, 1891, went into effect. In 1892, he, like the Green family and several other ranchers in the settlement, filed a deposition with the US Court of Claims. Marnoch petitioned for $9,060 in recompense for the value of a "large number of stallions, horses, mares, colts, and mules" stolen by Indians from 1869 through 1872. However, it would be years until such claims were settled, and for the most part, against the petitioners. What transpired instead was the revival of recollections of events that had occurred some twenty years before, among them the John Green killing.

When Will Green was elected constable of the precinct in 1892, he began visiting the old-timers in the community trying to learn the circumstances of his father's death. It is probable that he'd learned about the bounty Marnoch had put out for Menchaca after Menchaca had lassoed him and dragged him through town. It is also probable that Marnoch was not eager to go over that old ground. Dredging up the past was like poking a beehive: to get to the honey, you were likely to get stung.

Nevertheless, even without Marnoch's cooperation, Will had continued his quest for information, although nothing had come of his initial inquiry. But if Marnoch thought the case was closed, he underestimated the relentless quest for justice that propelled Will on behalf of his father. Now five years later and a deputy sheriff in San Antonio, Green had managed to revive the case, and Marnoch heard that witnesses were being summoned to appear before the grand jury to secure a new indictment for Menchaca.

Why couldn't the past just die?

Let us not go over old ground,
let us rather prepare for what is to come.
—Marcus Tullius Cicero, 106–43 BC

11

Old Ground

May 1897

The former Rangers stood in the second-floor corridor of the newly completed Bexar County Courthouse on Tuesday, May 25, 1897. Milling about the wainscoted six-foot-wide hallway, rich in dark wood and tiled floors, they admired the new four-story Romanesque building of red sandstone and granite. Careful not to discuss what transpired the day their sergeant was killed, the six witnesses wondered aloud about what had happened to their original testimony that had secured the first indictment all those years ago. Truth be told, the twenty-four intervening years had made the events of July 9, 1873, hazy, although the essential fact of the killing was not in question. Their conversation turned to their families, their farms, current events, and other remembrances of their Ranger days.

Francisco Rivas, sixty-seven, tall and lean, shoulders rounded from years of farm labor, was not happy to be there under the circumstances, but was pleased to see his old comrades. Frank Bihl had come the farthest, from his farm in Sutton County, almost two hundred miles away. That Will Green had managed that feat showed the lengths to which he would go to get Menchaca, which didn't bode well for Francisco's brother-in-law.

Taylor Jones farmed on the "dry Salado" in Bandera County, and Fritz Braun had a large spread in the Lockhill area of Bexar County close to Huebner's ranch. Both were married and had six children. Charlie Braun's property was in Helotes, where he ran cattle and farmed. He'd been constable of the precinct in the seventies, a position to which he'd been appointed after Menchaca's removal. Now Braun was considering a run for justice of the peace of their precinct, a position the popular rancher and father of ten would later win.

Jésus Zepeda was in a foul mood, not because of his upcoming testimony, but because a suit had been filed that very day in the Thirty-seventh District Court for a "writ of sequestration" on property his father and brother had purchased from rancher Jacob Hoffmann in 1884. Hoffmann, coincidentally a good friend of their late sergeant John Green, had accumulated more than ten thousand acres in northwest Bexar County over the years and was eager to acquire more. Hoffmann had fenced a portion of the Zepeda property and was using it as a cattle lease, disputing that he'd sold this section to the Zepedas and denying their claim for rent. The writ was issued to "preserve the named property pending outcome of the litigation."

All the men were sympathetic. Land disputes were common and costly, no matter who won the case.

Bihl, still the strapping man he'd been all those years before, had married Mrs. Sue Zimmerlie after a scandal in Castroville that involved court action against them for adultery and her subsequent divorce. Bihl also took in her two young boys to raise as his own. The youngest of the boys had died a few years earlier at age twenty-one, a great sorrow. But Frank and Sue were doing just fine with a growing brood of six children, primarily boys.

Rivas recalled that Bihl's parents had passed away when he was very young and he'd been sent to live at St. Mary's Catholic Boarding

School in San Antonio. Rivas had sent his own five youngest children to St. Joseph's Orphan Asylum in downtown San Antonio in November 1892, when it became too difficult to care from them after the death of their mother two years before. He'd been able to bring the three boys home in the fall of 1894, and then his eldest daughter a year later after she turned fourteen. But his youngest daughter was still at the orphanage. When she reached her fourteenth birthday in a couple of years, he'd bring her home. He consoled himself with the knowledge that she was receiving a good education.

James Van Riper and his brother William joined the men, although neither was on the witness list. Compelled by a bond that exists among any group of war veterans, they couldn't miss seeing so many from the old Minute Men Company together for the first time since disbanding twenty-four years previous. As chief deputy to the sheriff, James was a regular visitor to the county courthouse in any case. William Van Riper had opened a detective bureau a few years before and also had a commission as a "Special Ranger" for the State of Texas. In an April 13, 1897, letter regarding the sale of two of his bloodhounds, he mentioned that he was "thinking of going to Mexico," an indication that he might be part of the group to go after Menchaca if extradition papers were obtained.

One by one, each witness took his turn in the grand jury chamber as the others waited in the wainscoted hallway. Behind closed doors in front of a jury of twelve men and a felony prosecutor who questioned them, they told what they remembered about the day John Green died.

Deputy Will Green, acting as a bailiff for the May 1897 Thirty-seventh District Court term, a post he no doubt requested, watched as his father's old Ranger troop back-slapped and glad-handed each other and then stepped into the grand jury chamber. With the original indictment missing and a special session of the court coming up, Will had had to convince the district attorney to assign a new case number so that he could push forward with a new indictment and extradition.

The D.A. was willing if Will produced the witnesses. There was no statute of limitations for murder.

His father's old friends had not been eager to go over old ground; but in deference to Will, his law enforcement position, and the subpoena that threatened jail time if they didn't appear, they had no choice. After some time with Will, they began to relate details of some of their scrapes with Indians during their ten-day scouts, but would not discuss what happened the day his father died. Menchaca did kill him, they said, but there were a lot of things going on at the time. They wouldn't tell Will what the things were. They thought it best to let it come out in a trial.

Their camaraderie brought back memories of Will's childhood when the troop assembled at the Green ranch, that feeling of heady excitement as they joshed each other and teased him, and then the letdown of being left behind after they thundered off on their horses.

Will had been relentless in his quest to discover the identities of the original witnesses and then to subpoena them. He'd been fortunate to have the backing of his boss, Sheriff John Campbell, who was wholeheartedly behind Will's quest for justice. In fact, without the sheriff's approval, the case could not have progressed.

The next morning, Deputy Green took his place in the grand jury room as the foreman presented a bill of indictment based on testimony taken the day before. The indictment—*The State of Texas vs. Cesario Menchaca, for Murder, Case #13766*—simply stated, "Cesario Menchaca on or about the 9th day of July, 1873, and anterior to the presentment of this Indictment, in the County and State aforesaid, did, with malice aforethought, kill John Green, by then and there shooting the said John Green with a gun."

Short and to the point, the indictment was sufficient for the purpose of the exercise: to accompany a request to Texas Governor Charles A. Culberson for extradition papers for Cesario Menchaca. On the same day the indictment was handed down, a *capias* warrant was issued instructing "any Sheriff of the State of Texas" to bring in Cesario Menchaca to answer to the indictment "on or before the first Monday in October, 1897."

Bexar County District Attorney A. Lewy sent a letter and appropriate paperwork to the Texas governor on August 3, 1897, requesting his application to the governor of the State of Coahuila, Republic of Mexico, "for the apprehension and extradition of Cesario Menchaca to the United States." He recommended Campbell, sheriff of Bexar County, as the "proper person to be appointed and commissioned as the agent of the State of Texas."

Governor Culberson approved the application for requisition ten days later, on August 13, 1897, appointing Sheriff Campbell "to receive and return said fugitive, without any expense to the State of Texas under this appointment."

With a new case number for *The State of Texas vs. Cesario Menchaca* on the docket, the original case, #783, was dismissed on September 29, 1897. What happened to the original October 15, 1873, indictment is unknown, but a copy of it, which Deputy Green had not seen and apparently did not know existed, had been sent with a letter to the Texas governor in 1875, requesting the monetary reward for Menchaca's capture. The copy is on file in the Texas State Archives.

Although Deputy William F. Green had moved a huge step forward in his goal to bring Menchaca to justice, the struggle was far from over. For various reasons, likely starting with Sheriff Campbell's ill health, which included a bout with dengue fever, a viral infection transmitted by a mosquito bite, and other unknown delays, it would be another six years before the extradition papers were delivered to the Mexican government.

On March 11, 1901, after having resigned his position as a deputy sheriff, Will Green joined the San Antonio Police Department as a patrolman, serving under James Van Riper, who'd been appointed City Marshal, equivalent of Chief of Police. In the spring of 1903, after a change in administration, both Green and Van Riper resigned from the SAPD. Green ostensibly "went into the United States Secret Service." This time period coincides with Green's final push for extradition, although records could not be found for his employment with the federal government. It is plausible that Will used the ruse of this job to keep private his quest for Menchaca's extradition. While the ruse may have worked with local journalists, Menchaca's family was not so easily fooled.

12

Serving Citations

MAY 1903

Nine years older than Green, Lorenzo Morales, sporting a Kaiser-thick mustache, had an aura of authority not common among most Mexicans Will encountered. On a visit to Green's office in early May 1903, Lorenzo wore a dark suit and tie. A stiff derby upon his trimmed auburn hair also indicated his sense of decorum. Morales was polite, but not subservient. Will asked him to take a seat, which his guest did readily, removing his derby and placing it on the desk between them.

Will sat.

They gazed at each other in silence, both, it seemed, waiting for the other to speak. Will had learned over the years that the less he said, the more he learned. Morales seemed to be sizing him up, as if he weren't already acquainted with Will. They'd both grown up in the Helotes settlement. And although the Mexicans and Germans did not frequently socialize, educational and political concerns often brought them together.

Morales leaned forward, his blue eyes thoughtful. "I hear you are intent on extraditing my father-in-law from Mexico."

Will nodded.

"No good can come of it."

Will's jaw tightened.

"Cesario killed your father in self-defense." Lorenzo sat back.

"That's for a jury to decide."

"And do you want a jury to know that your father was a paid assassin?"

Will leaned forward, his hands gripping the desk. "Be careful what you say."

"It was Marnoch. He put a five-hundred-dollar bounty on Cesario's head."

Will stood. "Get out."

Lorenzo picked up his hat. He placed it on his head as he rose from the chair. Without another word, he walked out of the office, closing the door softly behind him.

Will sat back down.

He'd heard about Marnoch's bounty on Menchaca, but had not associated it with his father's death. Will believed in his father's integrity; in fact, he was invested in it. Nevertheless, he must have been consumed by doubts. Marnoch's defensive posture when Will had asked him if he knew anything about his father's murder now made sense. Will finally understood why his father's friends had been so reticent to tell him what happened. But did they actually believe John Green had intended to kill Menchaca for money, as Morales apparently did?

Whatever they thought, Will believed his father was no would-be assassin, and he would prove it the only way he knew how: arrest, extradition, jury trial, and, hopefully, conviction. He'd deliver the extradition papers to Mexican officials as planned, Morales's allegations be damned.

A man forewarned is equal to two.
                              —MEXICAN PROVERB

13

A Man Forewarned

MAY 1903

Cesario Menchaca walked outside the adobe farmhouse on the outskirts of the small village of Sabinas, Coahuila, where he and Magdalena had moved with their children several years before. The settlement on the railway line was twenty-two miles northeast of his hometown of Múzquiz, where they had lived when they first arrived in Mexico, and where Magdalena was now buried after a fatal bout of dysentery had taken her life two years before, in March 1901.

He lifted his hand to his brow to shade his eyes from the early morning sunlight and peered at the countryside by the Sabinas River, named for the cypress trees that graced its shorelines, where corn, beans, and sugarcane flourished. Sabinas station was a green oasis in the middle of an arid desert of cacti and agave. A train whistle broke the silence in the otherwise quiet community.

Now seventy-two, his hair the color of silver, Menchaca had spent the last thirty years of his life vigilant, the first five and the last five on high alert. His son-in-law Lorenzo Morales had written to him about John Green's son, now a law enforcement officer, and his quest to extradite Menchaca.

In the years since he'd fled Texas after he killed Green, Menchaca had become aware that as long as he was a fugitive from the law, he'd be able to relax completely only when he was caught or when he died. He looked forward to neither event, yet sometimes he yearned for just one moment of total freedom, the kind of liberty he'd felt before he killed his sergeant.

He'd been fortunate to have had the love and companionship of Magdalena, who'd given him a new family—in fact, five more children. His and Isabela's teenaged son, Donaciano, had come to Mexico to live with Cesario for a while, and they'd had a semblance of a relationship. But his daughters with Isabela had been lost to him. Cesario had missed the important occasions of his older childrens' lives: their weddings and the births of his grandchildren. And most sadly and profoundly, he'd missed their funerals. All but Emelia, his eldest daughter, had passed away: Victoria of consumption in 1888; Josefa, while still in the orphanage, had died in 1895; and then Donaciano died a year later.

Tears welled in his eyes. He swiped at the moisture as the sound of horses' hooves pounding on the ground grew louder and louder. He peered into the distance and saw a group of horsemen approaching the house. He recognized the chief of police and his deputies.

Menchaca's shoulders slumped, and he let out a big sigh as his son, Cesario Jr., emerged from the house and stood next to him. After thirty years, the fugitive's reckoning had arrived.

❧

Music, voices, and laughter—the sounds of fiesta—penetrated the thick walls of the Múzquiz municipal jail cell where Menchaca spent the night. The annual Cinco de Mayo celebration was already well underway at mid-morning in the plaza where vendors were preparing masa for tortillas and spicing meats to cook on makeshift grills. The smoky aroma of roasted goat wafted in through the small barred window, mingling with the stench endemic in jails: perspiration, urine, rodent droppings, and other foul odors.

His colonial hometown of 4,600, founded in 1739 as a presidio, would grow throughout the day as ranchers, farmers, miners, and workers from the large haciendas flooded in for the celebration, a one-day reprieve from the backbreaking and ill-compensated labor that was the story of their lives. Kickapoos from the Colonia del Nacimiento, a reservation in the Santa Rosa Mountains northwest of town, would bring their wares to sell in makeshift booths within the plaza.

Cesario leaned his thin frame against the thick adobe wall as he sat on his pallet on the concrete floor. His worst fear had come true and yet, he felt a great relief. Now that his past had finally caught up with him, he welcomed the chance to exonerate himself.

Menchaca was arrested on May 4, 1903, according to a telegram sent the next day to the governor of Coahuila from an official in Músquiz. His son, Cesario Jr., also sent a telegram to Governor Miguel Cardenas on his father's behalf. The message reiterated that the crime for which his father had been detained had occurred thirty years before and that Cesario was more than seventy years old. He further intimated that the laws of Mexico were in conflict with those of the United States and that Mexican law should prevail.

Menchaca's lawyer said that the legal aspects of the case looked good for Cesario and that he'd likely be granted bail after the hearing. That meant that besides a lawyer's fee, Cesario also needed bail money.

A small farmer with limited income and assets, Cesario considered whom he might call upon for financial help. His son-in-law Lorenzo, who lived in Texas, had recently remarried, and might balk at such a request from his former father-in-law. Certainly, his new wife would not be pleased. It pained Cesario to have to consider asking for money; nevertheless, he had no other choice. And there was something else: he'd never met Lorenzo, who had married his daughter Victoria, God rest her soul. He longed to know something of their lives in Texas during his long exile in Mexico.

— ❦ —

Clutching the telegram in his hand, Lorenzo Morales walked out of the Helotes General Store and Post Office wondering if the friendly glances and nods from other patrons masked an underlying suspicion. Six years after a new indictment and warrant were issued against Menchaca and extradition papers were approved by the governor, the Menchaca-Green case had been simmering like a disease in remission, ready to rear its ugly head at any moment. That moment had finally arrived. His father-in-law had been arrested.

Talk of the Green killing had been ongoing for several years. When Will and his younger brother, Johnny, first learned that Menchaca had killed their father, Johnny had confronted Morales, demanding his cooperation in bringing the fugitive back to Texas for trial, something Morales refused to do. Several men held Johnny back to prevent a fight. Will, known for his calm temperament, had taken another route. He'd become a peace officer, a much more effective path to bring Morales's father-in-law to justice, as today's telegram proved.

Morales hurried outside and mounted his horse for the five-mile ride on Bandera Road, a rutted and rocky dirt path forty feet wide, to his farmhouse northwest of downtown Helotes. There was no question that he would help Menchaca. In fact, he was eager to assist his former father-in-law, a legend in the family despite his thirty-year absence.

Morales had married Cesario's daughter, Victoria, in 1883. She died five years later. With her own mother long deceased and her father in Mexico, she'd requested on her deathbed that Lorenzo's parents and sister raise their two children, Juanita and Lorenzo Jr. Although Morales knew this arrangement was best, he often felt guilty even though he paid for the children's upkeep and visited them often on his relatives' adjacent farms. But when he heard Juanita call his sister

"Mama," it nearly broke his heart. This was surely not the life he'd dreamed of.

His new wife, Sulema Torres Lee, whom he'd married in the fall of 1902 upon the birth of their daughter Elvira, was a widow with several children. She had a strength of will and passion that were exciting, but which contributed to a volatile relationship (and a divorce a few years later). He did not relish having to tell her he was going to Mexico to assist his former father-in-law.

But Lorenzo was no coward. An imposing man and an avid equestrian, he'd inherited both his bearing and his horsemanship from his Spanish forebears, many, like him, blue-eyed with auburn hair. Born February 23, 1860, in the Presidio del Rio Grande where Santa Anna's army had crossed the river into infamy in 1836, Lorenzo had grown up with six siblings, all of whom had a knack with horses. But more important, they could all read and write, taught by their seminary-trained father.

After twenty-nine years in Texas, Lorenzo's English skills equaled his proficiency in Spanish. His Mexican neighbors, the vast majority illiterate and unable to understand English, often asked for help deciphering legal documents for land transactions, many, unfortunately, already signed and executed. Lorenzo enlisted the help of his older brother Mucio and a neighbor, J. N. Treviño, and started a legal aid society for the Mexican community.

In the years he'd lived in northwest Bexar County, little had changed. A few farmhouses stretched miles apart along Bandera Road. Undulating hills dotted with scrub oak and valleys sparsely cultivated with corn and other crops spread across the horizon. An occasional stone fence and long lines of barbed wire provided barriers for livestock. The Moraleses were relative latecomers, settling in the northwestern part of the county near a tributary of the Helotes creek called Los Reyes in 1874, a year after Cesario Menchaca killed Sergeant Green.

One of the first stories Lorenzo had heard upon arrival was about the killing. His cousin Jesús Zepeda Jr., eleven years his senior, had been in the Minute Men Troop with Menchaca and had been a witness to the shooting. Zepeda had tried to stop Cesario from running off, and had almost been shot himself.

Zepeda had told Morales that Gabriel Marnoch was involved, that he'd put a bounty on Cesario's head. But if Menchaca had been acting in self-defense, why did he flee to Mexico? It was a rhetorical question. Morales, although only fourteen, knew one thing definitively—Mexicans didn't get away with killing Gringos, especially a Gringo as beloved as Sergeant Green. Justice for Menchaca would have been at the end of a rope.

Morales recalled when, a few years later, Francisco Rivas had brought his nieces, Emelia and Victoria Menchaca, to live with him and his new wife on their San Geronimo farm in a settlement a few miles north of the Morales homestead. Emelia had been boarding at a Catholic convent in San Antonio, while Victoria and another sister, Josefa, were living in an orphanage, where Josefa remained.

Lorenzo was eager to see the daughters of the fugitive. The girls were lovely, refined, and of marriageable age. When Lorenzo saw Victoria for the first time, he set out to secure her heart. They married in 1883. Lorenzo's brother Cornelio married Victoria's older sister Emelia two years later, and the sisters' brother Donaciano married Eulalia Morales, the daughter of Lorenzo's older brother, Mucio, in 1893, another short-lived marriage interrupted by the young man's death in 1896.

The Morales and Menchaca clans were irrevocably connected, and Lorenzo was eager to help his father-in-law prove his innocence.

Truth suffers but never perishes.
—MEXICAN PROVERB

14

Truth Suffers

MAY 1903

On May 14, 1903, Cesario Menchaca was escorted from Músquiz to the northern border town of Ciudad Porfirio Díaz, now Piedras Negras, a distance of about 170 miles, for his extradition hearing in the Mexican Federal District Court. His lawyer argued "that the extradition petition [did] not meet the requirements of the applicable treaty or law." Menchaca's lawyer based his client's defense on several issues: Menchaca's contention that he killed Green in self-defense; incomplete extradition documents, including only one witness statement, that of Charles Braun; and the most compelling argument—that because thirty years had passed since the commission of the homicide of Sergeant Green on July 9, 1873, "the proscription against penal action would protect the accused, since after the elapse of 12 years, the law exempts even those crimes punishable by death," a precept reproduced in article III, section 3 of the Treaty of Extradition between Mexico and the United States.

The district judge agreed with Menchaca's lawyer, recommending that "extradition should not be conceded," and sent the petition and court proceedings to the president of the republic for a "definitive resolution" of the case. He also agreed to allow Menchaca out on bail pending the final resolution, just as his lawyer had predicted.

Lorenzo Morales walked across the iron bridge into Mexico at the port of Eagle Pass a few days after receiving a second telegram indicating that Menchaca was eligible for bail. The Rio Grande rushed underneath the 930-foot-long bridge, lapping the shoreline, swollen from recent heavy rains. The swirling waves reminded him of the whitecaps in Galveston where he'd been in charge of a crew that hauled granite from Marble Falls for the great sea wall after the devastating hurricane of 1900.

Ciudad Porfiro Díaz was a bustling border town of about five thousand, a population almost twice that of its American sister city, Eagle Pass, which had been founded in 1850 near the Army post of Fort Duncan. Despite a modern international railroad that connected the two countries over the imposing bridge, neither town had a street railway, nor a laid-out or graded road system. Tracks beaten down by wagons en route to market defined the roads. Indeed, it was difficult to differentiate one side of the river from the other; traditional Mexican buildings of adobe were the norm on both sides.

Morales stopped at the immigration and customs building before making his way to Hidalgo Plaza and the Presidencia jail, a straight shot down Juarez Street from the bridge, where his father-in-law had been transferred from the jail in Músquiz. During his two-block walk, Morales passed teams of horses, mules, and oxen hitched to wagons laden with corn, wheat, and other agricultural goods destined for export to the United States.

He approached the building of thick adobe and iron-barred windows, its entrance on Calle Iturbide. Two men in khaki uniforms and rifles stood guard at the imposing front entrance. Morales identified himself and was soon led into a small room, where he paid the requisite bail (in an unknown amount) and then waited while a guard went to collect his father-in-law. He paced back and forth, realizing for the first time that he was nervous.

A few minutes later, the guard returned accompanied by a thin, gray-haired man wearing a disheveled dark suit, his shoulders slightly stooped. His gray eyes watered as he gazed up at Lorenzo.

Menchaca opened his arms, and Morales, overcome with emotion, walked toward him. As they embraced, he heard Menchaca whisper, "Victoria, *mi hija.*" Tears ran down Morales's cheeks as they grieved together for the first time over the long-ago death of one man's daughter and the other's wife.

—•—

The Mexican International Railroad train left Ciudad Porfirio Díaz and ascended gradually toward Sabinas in the southwest, seventy-five miles distant. A hot wind blew through the open windows in the passenger car. Iron clattering on iron, chickens clucking in cages, and passengers shouting at each other over the noise provided a raucous backdrop to the men's conversation. The train traveled slowly, perhaps twenty miles per hour, ample time for Lorenzo to learn about Cesario's arrest, incarceration, and, most importantly, release from jail. Surely the case looked good for his father-in-law, or the judge would not have granted him bail.

After arriving at Menchaca's modest adobe home in Sabinas, Morales sat on the front porch with his father-in-law, where they awaited the preparation of a hearty midafternoon dinner prepared by relatives. Menchaca's children and grandchildren, nieces and nephews, cousins and friends had rushed over to see the patriarch. Raucous laughter and excited conversation followed news of his release and likely exoneration, and a party atmosphere prevailed. As the men relaxed on the porch, Menchaca's grandchildren urged him to show off his shooting prowess, which he agreed to do following retrieval of his rifle from the house.

"See the bird in that tree?"

Morales followed Menchaca's gaze to a tree about fifty yards away. Menchaca stood up, lifted the rifle, aimed, and pulled the trigger. The bird fell with a plop to the ground. Murmurs of approval erupted around them as one of the grandchildren ran to get the bird. After a few more demonstrations with bottles and other objects, Menchaca put the rifle down and his relatives began to scatter, the heaviness of the food in their bellies and the afternoon sun beckoning siesta.

After everyone had gone from the porch, leaving the two men alone, Menchaca interrupted the drone of cicadas. "You want to know what happened?"

Lorenzo looked at the old man and nodded.

Cesario sat back in his chair. "I was in law enforcement before I joined the Minute Men troop. I had a warrant to arrest Gabe Marnoch. I found him at the creek looking for frogs or lizards, something like that. He was a strange man.

"When I told him I had a warrant for his arrest, he got mad. Grabbed the warrant from me, tore it into pieces, and then threw it in the creek. Said he wasn't going to let no 'Meskin' arrest him. I lassoed him and walked him all the way to town. Later, I heard that he'd offered a five-hundred-dollar bounty for someone to kill me.

"Time passed and nothing happened. The Indians were raiding our ranches and I joined the Minute Men troop. Right away, Sergeant Green and I had problems. He treated me cold. We argued during one of our scouts and he told me he was going to throw me in the river. He didn't approve of the way I had arrested Marnoch. Other than that, he gave orders, expected them to be obeyed, and kept his distance.

"Our troop met once a month and went on scouts for Indians. My brother-in-law, Francisco Rivas, was in the troop. So was Jésus Zepeda. He was just a kid. We got to be good friends with some of the Germans in the troop. Frank Bihl, the Burell brothers. One day, one of the men, I can't remember which, told me to watch my back, that someone wanted to kill me.

"I was scared from that moment on. I kept thinking about Marnoch and his bounty on me. Maybe somebody wanted to collect.

"We always met a few days before the full moon for our monthly scouts. That July, we met on the eighth, a Tuesday, two days before the full moon. We met at Green's ranch and followed some Indian raiders, but they got away. We went back to the ranch and that night Sergeant Green put me on guard duty."

Menchaca paused. "The next morning, I went to relieve myself behind some bushes. When I came out of the bushes into camp, Sergeant Green and two others were waiting for me. I blurted out, 'Now is the time for you to kill me and throw me in the river like you said.'

"Green looked at me like he didn't know what I was talking about. I accused him: 'You want the bounty money.'

"He drew his gun, but I was faster." He paused. "When he fell to the ground, I realized what I had done. It was self-defense, but nobody would care. I killed Sergeant Green. People liked him. I was Mexican. I knew what would happen. I ran into the brush. I heard Zepeda call out my name. I turned around and saw him draw his gun. I shot in his direction. I didn't want to kill him, just wanted him to stay out of it."

"How did you get away?"

"I was on foot hiding behind some brush when I heard the horses. Bihl was the leader of one of the posses. He saw me and stopped. We looked at each other for a few seconds and then he ordered the riders in another direction."

"Why did he let you go?"

"He knew the sergeant and I didn't get along and he saw Green draw first." Cesario looked away, regret evident on his face.

Upon hearing Menchaca's story, Morales believed what had happened was a clear case of self-defense motivated by Green's attempt to kill Menchaca for Marnoch's alleged bounty. On the surface, the story seemed plausible, but was it true?

JULY 1903

In early July 1903, Cesario Menchaca was called back to Ciudad Porfirio Díaz for the final disposition of the extradition proceedings. The resolution, dated July 8—almost exactly 30 years to the day since the murder on July 9, 1873—and approved by President Porfirio Diaz, affirmed the findings of the District Judge of Coahuila and stipulated that Mexico would not "concede [to] the extradition of Cesáreo [*sic*] Menchaca solicited by the Government of the State of Texas, and to communicate to the District Judge of Coahuila that the prisoner be freed at once."

A little inaccuracy sometimes saves tons of explanation.
                                    —HECTOR HUGH MUNRO

A Little Inaccuracy

After thirty years as a fugitive from justice, Cesario Menchaca was free, although the extradition proceedings did not resolve the murder indictment against him in Texas. He was still unable to return under threat of arrest—his name, description, and crime had been included in the book *List of Fugitives from Justice for 1900*, published by the Texas Adjutant General's Department and used by law enforcement agencies for many years—but he was able to live with less anxiety in Mexico.

Cesario Menchaca died on January 7, 1910, in Villa de Sabinas, Coahuila. His death of *"cancer en la mano,"* or cancer of the hand, likely skin cancer, ended the longest-running murder indictment on Bexar County's 37th District Court Criminal Docket.

Will Green, who spent more than ten years attempting to bring his father's killer to justice, returned to the San Antonio Police Department as a mounted patrol officer on June 1, 1905. In September 1908, he was elevated to the position of detective in the SAPD. His stalwart stance for justice was mirrored again and again in his career. In 1927, when SAPD Chief of Detectives Sam Street was shot and killed in the line of duty, Green, appointed chief in his stead, told a *San Antonio Express* reporter, "one thing is for sure, and that is that I am going to rid San Antonio of all undesirable characters and wage relentless war against gunmen." He passed away on August 24, 1928.

James M. Van Riper and William H. Van Riper, who both served under John Green in Texas Ranger Minute Men Troop V of Medina County, had long law enforcement careers and were part of a family clan of officers that included brothers Garry Jr., Ed, and Frank. James became San Antonio's city marshal, equivalent to today's chief of police, serving from 1901 to 1903, and again in 1905. Both of his sons, Charles and Albert, followed him, serving as San Antonio police chief from 1908 to 1911 and 1922 to 1924, respectively.

William H. Van Riper's long law enforcement career included stints as a Texas Ranger, deputy US marshal, and general manager of the San Antonio Detective Bureau and Merchant Police Patrol, a position he held in the 1890s, along with a commission as a Special Ranger for the State of Texas.

Will Green's longtime friend and mentor, James M. Van Riper, whose favorite advice to young recruits was, "Now, boys, don't let the funeral happen on the wrong side," died of kidney failure on December 16, 1905, eleven days after resuming the position of SAPD chief of police. The mayor ordered the flag over City Hall to be lowered to half-mast upon hearing of Van Riper's death.

In Van Riper's *San Antonio Gazette* obituary, Will Green's father was mentioned: "At the close of hostilities [of the Civil War], he [Van Riper] joined a company of state rangers under the command of captain John Green of this city, and participated in many of the border encounters with the Indians and outlaws so numerous at that time."

Several years later, in another feature on the Van Riper law enforcement family, Green was again mentioned: "The Minute Men disbanded after the accidental slaying of John Green, the lieutenant of the company, and who led the men in their exploits."

The memory of John Green, actually commissioned as first sergeant and second in command of Minute Men Troop V of Medina

County, was kept alive in such published articles likely through the influence of his son, who remained close to the Van Riper family until his death.

The story of Cesario Menchaca's killing of John Green and Gabriel Marnoch's involvement in it was passed down in the Menchaca-Morales family through Cesario's son-in-law Lorenzo Morales, who heard it first-hand from Cesario himself after bailing him out of jail in Ciudad Porfirio Díaz, now Piedras Negras. Morales was a community leader who was a trustee for the Los Reyes School in the Helotes settlement for forty years, serving in that position alongside Gabriel Marnoch in the early part of his tenure.

The killing and extradition proceedings caused much turmoil in Helotes. When Lorenzo, who passed away on April 7, 1956, related the story to his children and grandchildren, he also admonished them to keep it to themselves. Many of Green's descendants still lived in the community and he didn't want to start another round of accusations and tension.

John Green's descendants were told that he was "killed by the Indians." It may be that Will and Johnny believed their father had indeed attempted to kill Cesario Menchaca for bounty money, or, more likely, because of the intricacy of the story, it was simply easier to attribute his killing to Indians.

By 1907, Gabriel Wilson Marnoch was living in greatly reduced circumstances. He'd sold much of the family land to pay off debts, including legal fees for his many brushes with the law. By 1889, the original 1,515-acre Marnoch ranch had dwindled down to 160 acres.

Prospective schoolteacher Armin Elmendorf described the house and grounds of the Marnoch homestead as a "gloomy sight of neglect" that made him "think of a story by Edgar Allan Poe," perhaps *The Fall of the House of Usher*. Since there was no hotel in the area and he'd arrived in Helotes for his interview for a teaching position in late afternoon, Elmendorf accepted Marnoch's invitation to stay the night. Frightened by the stories he'd heard about Gabriel, he "picked up some shears . . . to use as a weapon if necessary, and placed these under the pillow with the intention of remaining awake for the rest of the night." He fell asleep nonetheless, "accepting the hospitality of a presumed murderer!" The next morning, "Old Marnock rose at noon, wearing clothes he never changed for the night," and they left to visit the school.

Despite the "unsavory" stories that dogged Marnoch for much of his life, in scientific circles locally and nationally, he was acknowledged and respected for his work as a naturalist, although even Edward Drinker Cope considered him odd. In his diary, Cope wrote, "The M's are curious folk," referring to both Gabriel and his younger brother George. Nevertheless, Marnoch's reputation as a scholar seemed to override concerns about the transgressions of his youth. He was not only employed as a schoolteacher and as a school trustee, but in 1904 he was appointed Helotes postmaster, a position he held for fifteen years, and which was ironically the same position held by the man he'd killed in 1878. Marnoch was also a founding member of the Scientific Society of San Antonio, organized in 1904.

Other than the Morales family story regarding Marnoch's indirect role in the slaying of John Green, no written evidence has come to light of his having "put a bounty" on Menchaca; however, it would be unlikely that anyone, much less Marnoch, would put in writing something of this nature. It was illegal for private citizens to offer bounties for personal vendettas.

Those Marnoch descendants whom I was able to contact were not aware of the story of Gabriel's involvement in the Green killing and few knew of his documented killing of the town's postmaster. In one letter written to a relative by Gabriel's granddaughter Bernice Davis Russell, she wrote: "Wish I knew more; mom [Gabriel's youngest daughter Laura] was a secret person. She did not want anyone to know more than her."

Gabriel W. Marnoch passed away on February 4, 1920, at the age of eighty-three, ten years after the death of his nemesis Cesario Menchaca.

Writing this book was like putting together a puzzle without all the pieces. There is no definitive evidence about what happened the day John Green was killed, but after four years of intensive research into the story and the character of the individuals involved, I am convinced that his slaying was, as mentioned in the Van Riper article, "accidental," resulting from long-running tension between the two men over Menchaca's handling of the Marnoch case in particular, Menchaca's paranoia, and Green's incensed response at having his honor questioned.

The *San Antonio Daily Express* account of July 11, 1873, says: "Yesterday morning, Green ordered the camp to be removed to a point further west. While saddling for the removal, Menchaca suddenly shot Green dead with a Winchester rifle, another Mexican attempted to arrest him but he made his escape on foot to the brush after trying a shot at the other Mexican." The newspaper accounts in the *San Antonio Daily Express* and the *San Antonio Daily Herald*, though different in some aspects, both indicate that the slaying was sudden and occurred when the men were breaking camp. A person doesn't "suddenly" shoot another person without provocation, yet both newspaper accounts provide nothing more than speculation as to motive.

The *Daily Express* account mentions that Green had put Menchaca on guard duty for the night, and that Menchaca had failed to call "on the relief as was usual." The reporter went on to insinuate in his piece and in a second *Daily Express* article that Menchaca had been plotting with Mexican and Indian raiders during the night. This supposition is preposterous and likely put forth because Menchaca himself was Mexican by birth. Ethnic tension was high. Newspaper articles of this period invariably referred to those of Mexican heritage simply as "the Mexican," rather than by the individual's given name. An attorney for the United States Court of Claims in Marnoch's summary brief, published in 1916, complained about Marnoch's ten Mexican witnesses, writing, "The court has had considerable experience with Mexican witnesses in these Indian depredation cases and know that little reliance as a rule can be placed upon their testimony."

So why had Menchaca failed to call "on the relief as was usual"? Could it be something as simple as the fact that Menchaca had fallen asleep during his guard duty and the next morning Green found him snoozing and was justifiably angry? Sleeping while on guard duty, something that occurred more frequently than militarists would like to admit, was a serious infraction, punishable by court-martial, but more often through flogging or ridicule. After months of tension between the men, Menchaca, feeling defensive about his lapse, may have simply diverted the attention away from himself and confronted Green about Marnoch's bounty.

The *Daily Herald* account said that Menchaca was "considered not sound in the head," and may have "committed suicide," another erroneous assertion. Did one of Menchaca's fellow Rangers hint at a possible suicide to help Menchaca in his getaway?

Cesario's niece Matilde Menchaca, born a year after the slaying, wrote in her 1956 memoir that Cesario believed that "the captain wanted to kill him." She indicates that she heard this story from her father Miguel, Cesario's older brother.

She mentions that Cesario and Green (she doesn't mention his name in her narrative, referring to him as "captain" throughout) had had a conversation during which Green asked Cesario why he only arrested "Americans and not the Mexicans," and Cesario's response was, "Because the Mexicans are true gentlemen and the Americans are nothing but thieves and bandits." One of them "challenged a duel," they set a date for it, and Menchaca killed Green in this duel.

Lawrence Morales, Menchaca's great-grandson, who heard the story as presented in the last chapter from his grandfather Lorenzo, discounts Matilde's story of the duel. All the newspaper accounts also indicate that the killing was sudden. It also appears from what she wrote that Matilde was confused about Cesario's tenure as a constable and his later association in the Minute Men troop.

Her account does give credence to the ongoing animosity between the men, which Menchaca verified to Lorenzo, and one other important aspect of the slaying—the idea that someone's honor was impugned. The fact that Matilde used the word "duel" is significant. Duels were fought based on a code of honor, not so much to kill an opponent as to gain satisfaction, or restore one's honor.

Unfortunately, as Will Green discovered, eyewitness grand jury testimony no longer exists, so there is no other corroboration concerning what happened that day except for a copy of the original grand jury indictment at the Texas State Archives, which states that Cesario "feloniously, willfully and of his express malice aforethought did kill and murder [John Green]," and Cesario's version of events as told to the Mexican authorities during the extradition proceedings. His testimony, which survives as the only written evidence of motive, was that Sergeant Green attacked him and he responded in self-defense. What is not mentioned is why Green attacked him.

Another interesting aspect of this case is that there was no mention of the shooting in the newspapers after the few initial reports. A Bandera, Texas, resident wrote a letter to the editor of the *Daily Herald* about two weeks later speculating that Green had been felled "by the hands of a Mexican assassin, the accomplice, as we believe, of the Indians." This was the last mention of the Green slaying in any newspaper for several decades.

The Morales family story that several of the Germans in the troop helped Cesario escape gives credence to the belief that at least a few of his fellow Rangers believed Green did indeed attempt to kill Cesario for nefarious reasons and that Cesario was defending himself when the slaying occurred.

Later, when Will Green began the long process of fighting for Menchaca's extradition, there was no mention whatsoever of his quest in any newspaper. Extradition reports were few during that time period, but several were mentioned in local, state, and national newspapers. Even after the extradition papers were delivered and the extradition was denied, nothing appeared in newspapers. It was as if the case was of so little import that it didn't deserve mention. However, it could have been that Will Green kept this personal case private, choosing not to discuss it with newspaper reporters until and unless Menchaca's extradition was approved, a long shot as mentioned in the narrative.

My goal was to illuminate a time period painfully evolving from a chaotic frontier society to an era of law and order through the story of five very different men caught up in the struggle. Marnoch's interest in the natural sciences, a little-depicted topic in Western genre history, provided an interesting backdrop to an already compelling story.

Ultimately, I wanted to learn the truth behind the story of the killing of John Green. Despite discrepancies typical in oral histories, I learned that the "skeleton" of the narrative was accurate, which allowed me to put flesh on the story. My interpretation of events may also be faulty, but it was made only after exhausting myriad source materials. I was particularly impressed—even though the whole truth might never come to light—that the events leading up to the killing and its aftermath impacted so many lives. I came away from this book project with a deeper appreciation for our Texas pioneers and a profound respect for the storytellers who keep alive their families' important histories.

Author's Note

On Sunday, January 24, 2010, a Texas Ranger Memorial Cross ceremony honoring 1st Sergeant John F. Green was conducted at the Ballscheit Family Cemetery, adjacent to the Zion Lutheran Church, a parish that has served the Helotes community for more than a century. Sponsored by the Former Texas Rangers Association, the memorial cross is a fitting tribute for Green and a culmination of years of effort by his descendant, Shirley Green Sweet, who was given the task of not only keeping the family history alive, but to care for the Green family cemetery, which had fallen into disrepair and was eventually swallowed up in the expansion of San Antonio's boundaries.

I found Shirley through a 2005 article in a local alternative newspaper, the *San Antonio Current*, which had published a piece about Green's burial spot—under a front lawn in a San Antonio subdivision, about a half-mile from the original Green homestead. Although the developer had given the family an easement for the cemetery, which had three gravesites, vandals destroyed it before the subdivision was built, tearing down the tombstones and limestone block fence. The Sweets retrieved Green's tombstone and a few of the limestone blocks, but decided against exhumation of their ancestor's remains, a costly and likely unproductive affair. What happened to the other tombstones, one that marked the grave of Augusta's second husband Robert Robinson and the other of an unidentified family member, is unknown. In a gesture of goodwill, the developer of the French-named subdivision, Guilbeau Park, named the street where John Green was buried and remains interred Jean Verte.

The Ballscheit Family Cemetery is on another parcel of the original Green ranch. Green's memorial cross and a limestone commemorative marker from the Green cemetery are located behind the gravesites of

Green's wife, Augusta, who died in 1927, and her third husband Julius Ballscheit, who died in 1923.

Another point that piqued my interest in the article about Green's burial site was its assertion that Indians had killed Green, something I knew from my research was incorrect. When I contacted Shirley, the granddaughter of Green's son, John A. "Johnny" Green, and told her what I had learned, she was astonished. As long as she could remember, the Green family story passed down through the years was that Indians had killed John Green. She was also unaware that he was a Texas Ranger.

The "hidden" Green story, coupled with the Morales family story, and Marnoch's alleged involvement were a storyteller's dream.

To reconstruct the lives of the real people who populate this book, I spent countless hours in the archives of the Bexar County Records Department, the Bexar County Spanish Archives, the Texas State Archives, and the Texana/Genealogy Department of the San Antonio Public Library. I pored through numerous Indian depredation depositions from the US National Archives. I interviewed descendants of the main characters and of the members of the Minute Men Troop V of Medina County.

I used archival sources, official government records, maps, photographs, journals, first-person accounts, interviews, newspapers, and books. Everything that appears in quotation marks was taken from one of these sources and is indicated in the Notes section. In some cases, dialogue within quotation marks has been reconstructed from straight narrative; these sections are clearly denoted in the Notes section. In other cases, dialogue without quotes is used as a credible reconstruction of conversation. Such dialogue is used sparingly.

Reconstructing the life of Cesario Menchaca, especially after he fled to Mexico, was most challenging. Eventually, through genealogical research, civil and church records, legal records from government archives in Texas and Coahuila, Mexico, and family stories, I was able to trace his life as "a fugitive from justice" and construct a reasonable portrayal of the man. Unfortunately, I could locate no portrait of him, although his description—"height 5 feet 8 inches, weight 145 pounds, color light, complexion light, eyes grey, hair grey"—is in the *List of Fugitives from Justice for 1900*.

Gabriel Marnoch, because of his work as a naturalist and his many bouts with the law, left a clear record: a paper trail that allowed a fairly thorough depiction of him.

Johann Gruen/John Green's family has often been mistaken for another German immigrant family that settled in Fredericksburg. After careful analysis of the sources, I was able to distinguish his lineage and construct his life story.

On June 28, 1946, the US Court of Claims "disallowed" the Indian Depredation claim John Green's heirs had filed in 1892. The judgment came fifty-four years after the claim was filed and seventy-three years after Green's death. The claim for the loss of 105 horses valued at $4,560 had followed a tortuous path from dismissal because of Green's non-citizenship, to reinstatement, to request for dismissal for non-prosecution, to reinstatement, to transfer from the US Court of Claims to the American Mexican Claims Commission. The finding in the final judgment was that the claim did "not contain specific enough allegations of complicity or negligence on the part of Mexican authorities."

What likely kept the Green family moving forward was that some claimants had received settlements. In the three decades that the Court of Claims decided Indian depredation cases, 10,841 claims were adjudicated, and approximately $5.5 million was dispersed to about 3,600 claimants. The heirs of their father's friend, Jacob Hoffmann, who'd died in 1903, received a settlement in 1917, of $695, minus a $104 fee, on a $1,420 claim for forty horses. Although some heirs and estate administrators received rewards, "the biggest winners were the claims agents and lawyers."

The Indian depredation depositions make for interesting reading, and it's easy to see how so many claims that relied on this testimony were disallowed. The depositions were taken some twenty to forty years after the events, so inconsistencies abound in these accounts. Nevertheless, the depositions provided enough information to erect a foundation for this book. Family stories and oral history, while offering many elements of truth, were also conflicting. Even so, the essential elements of the Morales family story about Green's killing, retold for more than a century, have proven remarkably accurate.

Cynthia Leal Massey
Helotes, Texas

Acknowledgments

Many people assisted me as I gathered information for this book. First and foremost, I would like to thank Lawrence Morales and acknowledge the late Herlinda Ibarra, who kept alive the story of their ancestor Cesario Menchaca. I also thank Joseph Menchaca and Mary Esther Zahradnick for sharing their research materials on the Menchaca family. It would have been impossible to construct Cesario's life without their help. I'd also like to thank Shirley Green Sweet, who so graciously shared a suitcase full of memorabilia on her Green ancestors. Special thanks to Carolyn Kennedy, owner of the Marnoch homestead, who provided me with copies of letters and other documents relating to Gabriel Marnoch and his family.

I give my sincere thanks to those listed in the Sources section of this book who provided private papers and/or correspondence, and who gave of their time for interviews. I am especially grateful to those who provided photographs, especially Bradford Boehme who discovered the rare tintype of three members of Texas Ranger Minute Men Troop V of Medina County among items belonging to his ancestor Jacob Haby, and to Western artist and collector Donald Yena, to whom Brad entrusted the photograph.

I offer my sincere thanks to those who labor in the archives and reference departments of public institutions who were unfailingly professional and cordial when I made my myriad requests for materials, especially: Donaly E. Brice, Texas State Library and Archives Commission; Mary Frances Ronan, Federal Indian and Land Records, the National Archives and Records Administration; Frank Faulkner and Matt DeWaelsche, Texana/Genealogy–San Antonio Public Library; Kate Cordts, Interlibrary Loan–San Antonio Public Library; Stephanie Boothby, Daughters of the Republic of Texas Library; Trey Crumpton, Mayborn Museum, Baylor University; Paul D. Rivera,

Bexar County Records Center; Bro. Robert Wood, St. Mary's University Blume Library Special Collections; Alfred Rodriguez, Spanish Archives at the Bexar County Courthouse; Steven Kerr, Royal College of Surgeons of Edinburgh Library and Special Collections; Bro. Edward Loch, Catholic Archives of San Antonio; Candace Noriega, Pioneer Memorial Library, Fredericksburg, Texas; Ralph G. Serrano, Central Records & Identification Section, Bexar County Sheriff's Office; Christy Smith, Texas Ranger Hall of Fame and Museum, Waco, Texas; Beth Standifird, San Antonio Conservation Society; Anita Younes, former director of Historic Preservation and Decorative Arts at the Menger Hotel; Sr. Rosemary Meiman, Central Province of Ursulines; Debbie Elsbury, Blanco County District Clerk; Molly Cuellar, Medina County District Clerk; Clare Flemming, Academy of Natural Sciences Library & Archives, Philadelphia; and the staff of the *Archivo General del Estado de Coahuila*.

Thank you to Bob Battaglia, secretary/historian of the Coker Cemetery Association and steward of the association's website, which contains vast amounts of information on the Van Riper family. Thanks to Sean Walsh of the San Antonio Police Department who put me in contact with former San Antonio Police Chief William "Bill" Gibson, avid collector of law enforcement memorabilia. Bill kindly shared his research on the Van Riper brothers and pertinent photographs.

Special recognition goes to genealogists Wanda Qualls and Paula Sain. Qualls has done a lion's share of work on the families of Gillespie and Comal Counties, which are posted online. Sain saw my request for information on Gabriel Marnoch on Ancestry.com and did an extensive genealogical survey on the Marnoch family.

I am especially grateful to Dr. Florence Weinberg and my brother-in-law David Holgado, for translating several Spanish language documents into English, and to the Daedalus Critique Group—Irma Ned Bailey, Jim Peyton, Linda Shuler, Bill Stephans, Florence Weinberg, Diana Lopez, and Ralph Freedman—for reading and critiquing several drafts of the manuscript. Their observations were invaluable. I'd also like to acknowledge Women Writing the West, which provided the forum that secured me both an agent and an editor for this book.

I cannot go without thanking Mark Stepp, who told me that writing the history of Helotes would yield myriad stories, convincing me to embark on a new genre of writing. He could not have been more right. The late Claude Stanush, author of *The Newton Boys*, was very supportive of my work. I will be forever grateful for the kind letter he sent to me commending my primary research and writing.

I'd also like to acknowledge my friend and colleague, the late Charles H. Booker, a fine writer, who passed away as I was finishing this book. A few years ago, I asked him to locate the source of one of the quotes I wanted to use. He was an expert on research on the Internet, but my request stymied even him. Nevertheless, he finally found the original source of the quote by Sir Walter Scott, and even wrote a column about his search in the San Antonio magazine for which he wrote. The article is easy to find on the Internet. He was quite pleased when I told him I would make sure to acknowledge him in my book when it was published. Here is the acknowledgment, my dear friend. I didn't forget and I never will.

I am grateful to my family and friends for their support and forbearance over the several years it took me to write this book. To my agent, Sandra Bond, thank you for believing in me and in this story. Finally, special thanks to Erin Turner, an astute editor whose editorial direction has made this book fairly shine.

Notes

Part One and Two Epigraphs

Darwin, Charles. *The Origin of Species*, Barnes & Noble Classics, based on first edition published in 1859, New York, 2008, p. 60.

———. *The Descent of Man*, Vol. 1, D. Appleton & Company, New York, 1871, p. 86.

Preface

vii: *Old Man Marnoch . . . :* Morales, Lawrence. Interview. 11/15/2008. Morales is a great-grandson of Cesario Menchaca.

vii: *Father of American . . . :* Joseph Leidy Online Exhibit. The Academy of Natural Sciences of Drexel University. www.ansp.org/museum/leidy/index.php.

viii: *I inquired how . . . :* Elmendorf, Armin. *A Texan Remembers*, p. 22.

ix: *several hundred men . . . awakened interest in . . . :* Geiser, Samuel Wood. *Naturalists of the Frontier*, pp. 12, 17.

Chapter 1

3. *I sat up many nights . . . : Augusta Ballscheit, et al, vs. The United States and the Kickapoo Indians*, RG 123 Indian Depredations Claims, No. 7835, 2/10/1898, National Archives.

3. *firm title:* Pace, Robert E. and Donald S. Frazier. *Frontier Texas*, p. 145.

4. *Someone's after the horses . . . : Jacob Hoffmann vs. The United States and Kickapoo and Comanche Indians*, Indian Depredation Claims, No. 2891, deposition of Augusta Ballscheit, 9/23/1898, National Archives.

4. *Sounds like a hurt dog:* Ibid.

4. *Comanche:* Ibid.

5. *pulled it out: Jacob Hoffmann* . . . No. 2891, deposition of Juan Hernandez.

5. *sent word to the soldiers* . . . *: Jacob Hoffmann* . . . No. 2891, deposition of Augusta Ballscheit.

5. *We followed the trail* . . . *: Jacob Hoffmann* . . . No. 2891, deposition of Jacob Hoffmann.

6. *even in hot* . . . *; without the permission* . . . *:* Fehrenbach, T. R. *Lone Star: A History of Texas and the Texans,* p. 530.

6. *unscrupulous traders:* Pace, Robert E. and Donald S. Frazier. *Frontier Texas,* p. 144.

8. *suitable harbor; fresh water:* Geue, Chester William and Ethel Hander Geue. *A New Land Beckoned,* p. 5.

8. *approximately 3,800 died:* Biggers, Don H. *German Pioneers in Texas,* p. 36.

9. *like little wild Indians:* Mueller, Esther. "A Pioneer Wheelwright Shop, at Fredericksburg," *Frontier Times,* p. 538.

11. *"Stuttering Lane":* Hunter, J. Marvin. "Bladen Mitchell," *Pioneer History of Bandera County,* p. 22.

11. *clever:* Smith, Thomas T. *The US Army and the Texas Frontier Economy, 1845–1900,* p. 119.

12. *a Comanche warrior; arrows, bows, sundry* . . . *:* Berlandier, Jean Louis. *The Indians of Texas in 1830,* p. 99.

13. *Although the Germans* . . . *:* Curtis, Sarah Kay. Quoted in Johnson, Melvin C. *Polygamy on the Pedernales: Lyman Wight's Mormon Villages in Antebellum Texas, 1845 to 1858,* p. 88.

14. *have nothing more . . . :* Hunter, J. Marvin. "Elder Lyman Wight Brings His Colony to Bandera," *100 Years in Bandera, 1853–1953*, p. 3.

14. *sawing and grinding:* Johnson, Melvin C., p. 180.

14. *genial:* Hunter, "Bladen Mitchell," *Pioneer History of Bandera County*, p. 23.

15. *Between 1836 and . . . :* Fehrenbach, T. R., *Lone Star: A History of Texas and the Texans*, p. 280.

15. *for either conducting . . . :* Klos, George. "Indians," *Handbook of Texas Online* (www.tshaonline.org/handbook/online/articles/bzi04), accessed April 9, 2013. Published by the Texas State Historical Association.

16. *Comanches had stolen . . . :* Johnson, Melvin C., p. 184.

16. *Indians had stolen . . . ; which put idle . . . ; a few Rangers . . . :* Ibid.

16. *one of the bravest . . . :* "Letter from Bandera," *The Daily Herald*, San Antonio, 7/27/1873, p. 2.

16. *Injuns. Six miles. Kilt . . . :* This and dialogue that follows is dramatized from August Santleban's narrative in *A Texas Pioneer*, p. 20. One of Santleban's sons, Amos Graves, married Bertha Ackermann Green, stepdaughter of William Green, John Green's eldest son.

17. *the old South; with cotton planters . . . :* Fehrenbach, T. R., pp. 279, 281.

18. *economically unreasonable:* Ibid, p. 307.

18. *evil; foundation of democracy:* Marten, James. *Texas Divided: Loyalty and Dissent in the Lone Star State, 1856-1874*, 1990, p. 27.

19. *We [the former] . . . :* Johnson, Melvin C., p. 194.

19. *the response, by any . . . :* Fehrenbach, T. R., p. 354.

19. *who presented themselves for service . . . :* Smith, David Paul. *Frontier Defense in the Civil War*, p. 44.

20. *to act as a . . . :* Dunnam, Robert. "Frontier Regiment," *Handbook of Texas Online* (www.tshaonline.org/handbook/online/articles/qjf01), accessed April 11, 2013. Published by the Texas State Historical Association.

20. *as one of the blackest days . . . :* Knopp, Kenn. "The Massacre on the Banks of the Nueces," Book One, *German Immigration to America*, p. 120.

20. *to defend the neighborhood . . . :* Rodríguez, José Policarpo. "The Old Guide," *Old West* magazine, Winter, 1968, p. 92.

21. *He was a fearful-looking object . . . :* Ibid. This and dialogue that follows is dramatized from Rodríguez's narrative.

23. *he went out; that the same Indjans . . . :* Day, James M. and Dorman Winfrey. "Record of Indian Depredations in Bandera County [June 25, 1867]," No. 150, *Texas Indian Papers, 1860-1916*, pp. 225-26.

23. *very fine blood: Augusta Ballscheit, et al, versus The United States and the Kickapoo Indians*, RG 123 Indian Depredations Claims, No. 7835, Deposition of Charles Scheidemantel, 2/10/1898, National Archives.

Chapter 2

27. *But I was born a Scotchman . . . :* Sir Walter Scott, from a letter to J. B. S. Morritt, March 2, 1810. Quoted in full in J. G. Lockhart's 1837 biography of Scott. In the twentieth century, the quote was shortened and paraphrased by subsequent biographers.

27. *strange faces . . . at every corner:* "Local News." *The Daily Herald,* San Antonio, 9/11/1858, p. 2.

27. *the place, for capitalists . . . :* Ibid.

28. *bought at very reasonable rates:* "San Antonio," *The Daily Herald.* 8/31/1858.

29. *Lands, City Lots, Negroes . . . :* Advertisement. *The Daily Herald.* 10/1/1858, p. 1.

29. *the bat cave:* Santos, Sylvia Ann. "Courthouses of Bexar County, 1721–1978."

30. *lung ailment:* Van de Walle, Lorraine. Telephone interview, 8/5/2006. Van de Walle was the granddaughter of Gabriel W. Marnoch. She passed away 10/9/2009 at the age of eighty-four.

31. *in this enlightened age . . . speculations upon the . . . :* "Comets." *The Daily Herald.* 10/5/1858.

32. *all seeming disposed to applaud . . . :* "Opening of the Menger Hotel." *The Daily Herald.* 2/1/1859.

32. *furnishing of lumber or . . . :* John Fries vs. G. F. Marnoch. No. #2617. Contract. 1/24/1859, Bexar County Civil Records.

33. *at his own risk:* Ibid. Letter from Marnoch's attorney. 6/11/1859.

34. *Mr. Fries warranted that the chimneys . . . :* Ibid. Bexar County Court petition. 4/21/1860.

34. *substituted lintels for . . . :* Ibid.

34. *short arms and deep pockets:* "Edinburgh." DVD. *Rick Steves' Ireland and Scotland.*

35. *repulsed by surgery:* Kennedy, Robert C. "The Darwinian Student's After-Dinner Dream," *HarpWeek*, New York Times Company, 2001.

35. *considerable correspondence . . . :* Elmendorf, Armin. *A Texan Remembers.* p. 23.

36. *duly authorized agent: A. & A. G. McClung vs. G. W. Marnoch, et al,* No. 3785. Bexar County Civil Court Petition, 8/24/1867.

37. *foreign vessels bound . . . :* Becker, Jack and Matthew K. Hamilton, "Wartime Cotton Trade," *Handbook of Texas Online* (www.tsha-online.org/handbook/online/articles/drw01), accessed April 15, 2013. Published by the Texas State Historical Association.

37. *that had done . . . : Caroline Huebner, et al vs. The United States,* Indian Depredation Claim, No. 7891. Gabriel W. Marnoch deposition, 11/26/1914. National Archives.

37. *proved very trustworthy:* Ibid.

37. *fraudulently embezzling: A. & A. G. McClung vs. G. W. Marnoch, et al.*

38. *were not Mexican: Caroline Huebner, et al vs. The United States.*

38. *they had been captured:* Ibid.

38. *welcome to them:* Ibid.

38. *the offence of . . . :* Scire Facias Writ, José Angel Torres and J. F. Marnoch, *The State of Texas vs. Gabriel Marnoch*, No. 320, 11-24-1871.

40. *Mr. Marnoch, I have a . . . :* Morales, Lawrence. Interview, 11/15/2008. See also Bexar County Records Archives. *Journal "A" Criminal Minutes 1869–1873, The State of Texas vs. Gabriel Marnoch*, Issuance of arrest warrant, 11/13/1871. See also Bexar

County Spanish Archives. *Commissioners Court Minutes*. Cesario Menchaca appointed Constable, 10/2/1871.

40. *No Meskin's gonna . . . :* Ibid.

Chapter 3

41. *Who overcomes by force . . . :* Milton, John. *Paradise Lost*, Book I, Line 648.

44. *put a bounty . . . :* Morales, Lawrence. Interview, 11/15/2008.

45. *quash the indictment:* The State vs. Gabriel Marnoch, #320, *Criminal Journal*, Bexar County District Court, 4/4/1872, p. 242.

45. *about $300:* "Local News: District Court," *The Daily Herald*. San Antonio, 4/6/1872.

45. *With that money . . . :* Ibid.

45. *failed to qualify:* Bexar County Commissioners Court Minutes, Book A3, August 1868–July 1876, 5/27/1872, p. 314.

45. *one of the most horrible . . . :* "An Indian Massacre," *The New York Times*, 5/18/1872.

46. *Indians, Mexicans, and deserters . . . :* Ibid.

46. *brains dashed out:* Ibid.

46. *horribly bloody, mutilated . . . :* Fehrenbach, T. R., *Lone Star*, p. 539.

46. *in return for peace; under no conditions . . . :* Ibid., p. 541.

46. *When I formerly . . . :* Letter to the Editor, *The Daily Express*, San Antonio, 8/21/1872.

47. *Considered Rangers, the . . . :* Wilkins, Frederick. *The Law Comes to Texas: The Texas Rangers, 1870–1901*, p. 16.

Chapter 4

49. *I do solemnly swear . . . . :* Jno [*sic*] B. Jones signed oath of office for service in the Texas Ranger Frontier Battalion, 5/19/1874, Texas State Archives.

49. *in Boerne, Texas*: "Leopold Haby," *Pioneer History of Bandera County*, p. 146.

50. *fighting Habys:* "Joseph George Haby," *Medina County History*, p. 302.

51. *In every engagement . . . :* "Famous Family of San Antonio Peace Officers Helps Make Texas History," *San Antonio Evening News*, 3/28/1924, p. 17.

51. *short [and] stout:* "George Haby," *Medina County History*, p. 302.

52. *Hey there, Runaway . . . :* Joseph M. Burell obituary. Burell file at Texas Ranger Museum Library, Waco, Texas. Dramatized dialogue.

53. *hair breath escape; Runaway Mike:* Ibid.

53. *In mid-September: Thebolt Monier vs. The United States*, Court of Claims, No. 7488, Deposition No. 923, T. Monier, 5/17/1873.

53. *Under the above . . . :* Veritas, Letter to the Editor. *The Daily Herald*, 10/20/1872.

54. *better frontiersman; went ahead and . . . : Augusta Ballscheit . . .* No. 7835, Deposition of James Van Riper.

54–55. *with a partner . . .; blooded horses:* "Famous Family of San Antonio Peace Officers Helps Make Texas History," *San Antonio Evening News*, 3/28/1924, p. 17.

55. *nights of terrifying . . . :* Ibid.

55. *especially anxious to . . .; that a man . . . :* Anton Gugger, Letter to the Editor, *The Daily Herald*, 10/18/1872.

56. *Had a feast:* Leopold Haby.

56. *the old Indian . . . ; secure sleep and rest . . . :* Ibid.

56. *either Kickapoo or . . . ; 100 head of horses . . . : Augusta Ballscheit . . .* No. 7835, deposition of James Van Riper.

57. *had made good . . . :* Leopold Haby.

57. *They [the Indians] . . . :* Anton Gugger.

Chapter 5

59. *Left to themselves . . . :* Woodbury (1855–1930) was an American author, educator, and poet who was famous for his aphorisms.

59. *based upon a . . . :* "Grant's Indian Policy," *San Antonio Daily Herald*, 11/10/1872.

59. *company performed ten . . . :* Muster and Payroll, December 1872, Minute Men of Medina County, Company V, Texas State Library and Archives Commission.

60. *first light moon:* Gillett, James B., *Six Years With the Texas Rangers*, p. 34.

60. *bad feelings:* Menchaca, Matilde. "Tia Mencha's Story." Unpublished memoir of Matilde Menchaca, 1/1/1956.

61. *coughed and spit . . . : State of Texas vs. Julius Heuchling*, Case File No. 520, Medina County District Court, Archives, deposition of Joseph Koenig, 3/18/1873.

61. *I was very drunk: State of Texas vs. Julius Heuchling . . .* voluntary statement of Julius Heuchling, 3/18/1873.

61. *Haby expelled him....:* Although the muster records for Troop
    V list Heuchling as having served the entire term the troop was
    together, it is my belief that he did not for the reason stated in
    the text. Many of the muster records were reconstructed several
    years after the troop was in service, and this would also explain
    August Wurzbach's affidavit saying that in addition to substitut-
    ing for his brother in March, he served in his own name from May
    until August, 1873, although his service is not noted in the muster
    records. It is my contention that he served in place of Heuchling.

61. *languished in jail....:* Heuchling got out of jail on a $750 bond
    on March 18, 1873. At his October 15, 1873, trial with plaintiff
    Koenig, Heuchling was found guilty of simple assault and was
    assessed one dollar. At the trial with plaintiff Smith (Case 521)
    held the same day, he was found guilty of assault and battery and
    was fined one dollar. His former sergeant, Adolph Wurzbach, was
    the foreman of the Smith jury.

62. *band of thieves....: Report of the Adjutant General, 1873,* Appen-
    dix, page 122.

62. *charge of adultery: State of Texas vs. F. Beal* (sic), Case No. 566,
    Adultery with Sue Zimmerlie," Medina County District Court,
    1873-1875 (cont.)

62. *The Indians killed....:* The killing of the Joseph Moore family is
    well documented in Bandera County history books; however, the
    date of their death as published in some books (July 4, 1872) is
    incorrect. August Santleban in his memoir, *A Texas Pioneer,* pub-
    lished in 1910, places this family's demise in 1867. See page 267 of
    his book. This date is incorrect as well. The couple was killed Sun-
    day, July 6, 1873. See "Indians! Indians," a letter to *The Daily Her-
    ald,* July 11, 1873. This letter from Bandera resident J. B. Langford
    details the death of Joseph Moore, which he says occurred a few

days before, on Sunday, July 6, 1873. See also "Letter from Bandera" in *The Daily Herald*, dated July 26, 1873, which also confirms the July 6, 1873, death of Joseph Moore and his wife.

63. *the grateful thanks . . . :* Handbook of Texas online, s.v. "Remolino Raid."

63. *dropped the matter:* Ibid.

63. *information had been . . . :* "Our Indian Troubles," *San Antonio Daily Express*, 7/13/1873, p. 3.

Chapter 6

65. *And so the . . . :* Murder Indictment, No. 783, *The State of Texas vs. Cesario Menchaca*, from Governor's Rewards file, Cesario Menchaca 1875, holdings of the Texas State Archives.

66. *collusion:* "Local News," *San Antonio Daily Express*, 7/12/1873, p. 3.

66. *was not sound . . . ; committed suicide:* "Indians Becoming More Daring," *San Antonio Daily Herald*, 7/11/1873, p. 3.

66. *on the left . . . ; mortal wound of . . . :* Murder Indictment, No. 783, Ibid.

66. *suspended from duty; killed July 14; deserted July 14 . . . :* Muster and Payroll, July 1873, Minute Men of Medina County, Company V, Texas State Library and Archives Commission.

67. *no man, who . . . :* "Letter from Bandera," *San Antonio Daily Herald*, 7/26/1873, p. 2.

68. *not in accordance . . . :* "Texas Frontier Troubles," A Report of the Permanent Committee Appointed at a Meeting of the Citizens of Brownsville, Texas, 4/17/1875, Congressional Volume 1709, 1876, p. 51.

69. *abandoned his pre-emption....*: Affidavit of Abandonment, Bexar Pre-emption, Abstract 541, Grantee: Cesario Menchaca, Texas Government Land Office, Land Grants, filed 1/30/1878.

69. *on the Rio Grande....*: Letter from M. G. Anderson to Texas Governor R. B. Hubbard, 7/28/1877, from Governor's Rewards file, Cesario Menchaca 1877, holdings of the Texas State Archives.

69. *Due to our....*: Rewards, Executive Office, Subject Matter, Increasing Reward for Cesario Menchaca, etc., Answered 8/8/1877, Cesario Menchaca 1877, holdings of the Texas State Archives.

Chapter 7

71. *The only sure....*: Bret Harte, from his short story "The Outcasts of Poker Flat," 1869.

71. *theft of a mare:* *The State of Texas vs. Gabriel Marnoch*, No. 82, Kendall County District Court Minutes, 4/8/1875, p. 222.

72. *on an extended....*: Marnoch, G. W., Letter to Professor Leidy, 2/11/1877, Academy of Natural Sciences, Philadelphia, Archives Collection 567, Box 22, Folder 7.

72. *camp outfit:* Cope, Edward Drinker. Quoted in *Cope: Master Naturalist* by Henry Fairfield Osborn, Princeton University Press, 1931, p. 236.

73. *"inheritance of acquired...":* Othniel Charles Marsh (1832–1899), www.ucmp.berkeley.edu/history/marsh.html.

73. *the latter consisting of....*: Darwin, Charles. *The Descent of Man*, Vol. 1, New York: D. Appleton & Company, 1871, p. 96.

73. *bitter competition for....*: Osborn, Henry Fairfield. Quoted in *The Bone Sharp: The Life of Edward Drinker Cope* by Jane Pierce Davidson, Academy of Natural Sciences of Philadelphia, 1997, p. 74.

73. *he placed the head . . . :* Marsh, O. C. "Reply to Cope's Explanation," Appendix to *The American Naturalist*, Vol. 7, June 1873, p. ix.

73–74. *practically virgin fields . . . :* Osborn, Henry Fairfield. *Cope: Master Naturalist*, Princeton University Press, 1931, p. 233.

74. *a Mexican named . . . :* Cope, Edward Drinker. Quoted in *Cope: Master Naturalist* by Henry Fairfield Osborn, Princeton University Press, 1931, p. 237.

74. *miserable black horse; saddle . . . very dilapidated; mere 'crow baits'; lying on a table . . . ; pulled down a . . . :* Ibid.

74. *pitched out head . . . :* Ibid, p. 239.

74. *fossiliferous strata:* Ibid.

74. *from a zoological . . . ; wild beast large . . . ; fine [peccary]:* Ibid, p. 240.

75. *a new genus of . . . :* "Editor's Scientific Record," *Harper's Magazine*, Vol. 57, Issue 337, New York: Harper & Brothers, Publishers, June 1878, p. 155.

76. *turtle remains; ruins:* Marnoch, G. W., letter to Professor Leidy, 1/29/1877, Academy of Natural Sciences, Philadelphia, Archives Collection 567, Box 22, Folder 7.

76. *charging him with . . . :* G. W. *Marnoch vs. The State.* Appeal from the District Court of Bexar, *Cases Argued and Adjudged in the Court of Appeals*, 1879, Vol. VII, p. 273.

76. *I know you've . . . ; You're a liar:* Ibid. This dialogue is dramatized from narrative.

76. *recommenced abusing . . . ; very soon . . . ; they would fight . . . ; advanced upon him . . . ; holding his gun . . . ; stand back:* Affidavit for Continuance. *The State of Texas vs. G. W. Marnoch*, No. 494, 11/16/1878, Bexar County District Court, Records Center, San Antonio, Texas.

Chapter 8

81. *Where ignorance . . . :* "Ode on a Distant Prospect of Eton College" (1742).

82. *tough fighter and a good shot:* William A. Keleher. *The Fabulous Frontier: 1846–1912,* p. 372.

82. *typical Western cowboys:* "Charged with Robbing a Bank," *San Antonio Daily Express,* 3/20/1900, p. 7.

82. *Wilson, you and . . . :* Ibid.

85. *You shot a . . . :* Charles Kuentz Jr. interview, 7/21/2011.

85. *Comanche remnants:* Fehrenbach, T. R., *Lone Star: A History of Texas and the Texans,* p. 550.

85. *lynching:* "The Murder of Charles Miller [*sic*]," *San Antonio Daily Herald,* 3/20/1878.

86. *for the purpose . . . : The State of Texas vs. Cesario Menchaca,* No. 494, Affidavit for Continuance, Bexar County District Court, May 13, 1878, Bexar County Records/Storage Division, San Antonio, Texas.

87. *famous as a breaker of . . . :* "Capt. Green Named Street Successor, on Force 26 Years," *San Antonio Express,* 9/15/1927, p. 1.

87. *small, patently sound . . . :* All quoted material in this paragraph is from Rollins, Philip Ashton, *The Cowboy,* p. 207.

87–88. *throw a lasso . . . ; young man dressed . . . ; Suppose you put . . . ; make a running . . . ; found himself tied . . . : Deacon Green; pious appearance:* "Will Green Accommodated," *San Antonio Light,* 12/30/1906, p. 7.

88. *fleetness of foot . . . :* "Stevens Makes Capture after an Exciting Chase," *San Antonio Light,* 3/4/1908, p. 5.

88. *When Will Green . . . :* "Negro Qualifies for Track Work, He Outfoots Detective Green," *San Antonio Light and Gazette,* 12/4/1910, p. 26.

89. *refugee from justice . . . :* Elmendorf, Armin. *A Texan Remembers,* p. 22.

89–90. *festive . . . :* "City Local News," *San Antonio Daily Light,* 9/11/1891.

90. *in amity:* US Dept. of the Interior, *Federal Indian Law,* p. 457.

Chapter 9

93. *Revenge is a . . . :* A modern permutation of "revenge is not easily taken in cold blood," from *El ingenioso hidalgo don Quixote de la Mancha,* Chap. LXIII, by Miguel de Cervantes, 1615, translated by John Ormsby, 1885.

94. *Last order . . . :* Case 783, *The State vs. Cesario Menchaca,* Bexar County Judge's Criminal Docket, 37th District Court, May Term 1893, p. 89.

95. *strict officer:* "Many Auto Thefts Solved," *San Antonio Evening News,* 3/6/1919.

95. *If Ybañez is . . . :* "Taking Testimony–Proceedings in Carmen Ybañez's Case in Progress," *The San Antonio Daily Express,* 7/1/1892, p. 1.

95. *revolutionist:* "Carmen Ybanez Discharged," *The New York Times,* 7/11/1892.

96. *three main railroad . . . :* "Interesting Dates in the History of Old San Antonio—12/ 31/1890," San Antonio Notes. Collection in the Center for American History, the University of Texas at Austin.

96. *roared that San Antonio . . . :* Panfeld, Peter M. *Wild Nights and Roaring Days in Old San Antonio,* 1968.

96. *opium dens operated . . . :* San Antonio Notes, Collection in the Center for American History, the University of Texas at Austin.

96. *one of the most . . . :* All quoted material in this paragraph is from *A Twentieth Century History of Southwest Texas*, Vol. 1, 1907, p. 327.

96. *political:* "Extradition Refused," *The Galveston Daily News*, 7/28/1895, p. 4.

97. *capable administrator:* Gill, Andrews. "Bexar County Judge Robert B. Green, 1865–1907." www.bexar.org/commct/cmpct4/History/ Elected_Officials/Past_County_Judges/Robert_B_Green/ robert_b._green.htm. Accessed 1/31/12.

97. *some of them . . . ; among the number:* "Will Be Tried For Their Lives," *The San Antonio Daily Express*, 8/24/1897, p. 6.

Chapter 10

99. *Man . . . cannot learn . . . :* Nietzsche, Friedrich Wilhelm. *The Use and Abuse of History*, Liberal Arts Press, 1873, reprint edition, Cosimo, Inc., 2005, p. 5.

99. *old books that . . . :* Elmendorf, Armin. *A Texan Remembers*, 1974, p. 22.

100. *important specimen:* Cope, Edward Drinker. "On the Extinct Cats of America," *The American Naturalist.* 11/26/1880, p. 857.

100. *the ground seed . . . :* Report of the Commissioner of Agriculture for the Year 1880, US Department of Agriculture, p. 494.

101. *an abrupt elevation:* Cope, E. D. Quoted in Hill, R. T. "Texas Section of American Cretaceous," *The American Journal of Science*, July to Dec. 1887, p. 292.

101. *large number . . . : Gabriel W. Marnoch v. The United States and the Kickapoo, Comanche, and Kiowa Indians*, #3709, brief regarding

three depositions, the Court of Claims of the United States, Indian Depredations, Filed 7/25/1916.

Chapter 11

104. *dry Salado:* Indictment, *The State of Texas vs. Cesario Menchaca,* No. 13766, Name of Witnesses Upon Whose Testimony Indictment Was Found," 5/26/1897, Texas State Archive, Extradition Records, Cesario Menchaca, 1897.

104. *writ of sequestration:* "Court Record," *San Antonio Daily Express,* 5/26/1897.

104. *to preserve the . . . :* USLegal.com Definitions: "Writ of Sequestration," definitions.uslegal.com/w/writ-of-sequestration.

105. *Special Ranger . . . :* Mabry, W. H., letter to W. H. Van Riper, 9/23/1897, Texas State Archives, Texas Adjutant General Service Records, Frontier Battalion, William Van Riper, Call No. 401-175.

105. *thinking of going . . . :* Van Riper, W. H., Letter to Mr. J. Press Lane, 4/14/1897. William Gibson private collection.

106. *Cesario Menchaca on . . . :* Indictment, *The State of Texas vs. Cesario Menchaca,* No. 13766, 5/26/1897, Texas State Archives, Extradition Records, Cesario Menchaca, 1897.

107. *any Sheriff of . . . ; on or before . . . : Capias* Warrant, *The State of Texas vs. Cesario Menchaca,* No. 13766, 5/26/1897, Bexar County Records & Storage, 37th Judicial District, San Antonio, Texas.

107. *for the apprehension . . . :* Lewy, A., letter to the Hon. Chas. A. Culberson. Texas State Archive, Extradition Records, Cesario Menchaca, 1897.

107. *proper person to . . . :* Ibid.

107. *to receive and . . . :* Extradition Requisition, Department of State, No. 3315, 8/13/1897, Texas State Archive, Extradition Records, Cesario Menchaca, 1897.

108. *went into . . . :* "S. A. Detective Chief Fights Death," *San Antonio Light*, 8/21/1929, p. 2.

Chapter 12

109–10. *I hear you want . . . Get out:* Interview with Lawrence Morales, May 20, 2006. The precise date and place of the meeting between Will Green and Lorenzo Morales are unknown. I have chosen to place it before Menchaca's arrest and at Green's office as the most logical time and place for the conversation to have occurred. Lorenzo made frequent trips to San Antonio and Green lived and worked there after 1895.

Chapter 13

115. *Mama:* Interview with Herlinda Ibarra (Juanita's daughter), 5/23/2006.

Chapter 14

117–18. *that the extradition . . . ; the proscription against . . . ; extradition should not . . . ; definitive resolution:* Translation of "Acuerdo," correspondence regarding Cesáreo [*sic*] Menchaca, México. 8 de Julio de 1903. Fecha: 18 de Mayo de 1903. AGEC, FSXX, C13, F11, E7, 4F, Población: Músquiz. Al Archivo General del Estado de Coahuila, Saltillo.

119. *Victoria, mi hija:* Interview with Herlinda Ibarra.

120–21. *See the bird . . . He knew the sergeant . . . :* Lawrence Morales and Herlinda Ibarra interviews and newspaper accounts. See the Epilogue for more information.

122. *concede [to]the extradition* . . . : Translation of "Acuerdo," correspondence regarding Cesáreo [*sic*] Menchaca, México, 8 de Julio de 1903. Fecha: 18 de Mayo de 1903. AGEC, FSXX, C13, F11, E7, 4F, Población: Músquiz. Al Archivo General del Estado de Coahuila, Saltillo.

Epilogue

123. *A little inaccuracy* . . . : Hector Hugh Munro (1870–1916) was a British writer who wrote under the pen name Saki. This is quoted from "Romance of Business," *The Square Egg and Other Sketches with Three Plays*, by Saki and J. C. Squire, 1924, Kessinger Publishing, 2005, p. 136.

123. *cancer en la mano:* Death Certificate of Cesáreo [*sic*] Menchaca, Villa de Sabinas, Mexico.

123. *one thing is* . . . : "Capt. Green Named Street Successor, on Force for 26 Years," *The San Antonio Express*, 9/15/1927, pp. 1, 5.

124. *Now, boys, don't* . . . : "Veteran Ranger Protects Border," *The State Trooper*, 9/1924, p. 14.

124. *At the close* . . . : "J. M. Van Riper City Marshal Passes Away," *San Antonio Gazette*, 12/16/1905, p. 1.

124. *The Minute Men* . . . : "Famous Family of San Antonio Peace Officers Helps Make Texas History," *San Antonio Evening News*," 3/2/1924, p. 17.

125. *killed by the Indians* . . . : Elvie Green Pyka (1897–1993) taped interview by grand-niece Shirley Green Sweet on 4/15/1978. Pyka was the eldest child of John Green's son, Johnny Green. Pyka was close to her grandmother Augusta, who passed away in 1927. Augusta told Pyka that her grandfather was killed by the Indians.

125–26. *gloomy sight of* . . . ; *think of a* . . . ; *picked up some* . . . ; *accepting the hospitality* . . . ; *Old Marnock rose* . . . ; *unsavory :* Elmendorf, Armin. *A Texan Remembers,* memoir privately published in 1974.

126. *The M's are curious* . . . : Henry Fairfield Osborn, *Cope: Master Naturalist,* Princeton University Press, New Jersey, 1931, p. 237.

126. *Wish I knew more* . . . : Letter to Anita Marnoch Campbell from Bernice Davis Russell, 1/24/1994 (Carolyn Kennedy Collection).

127. *Yesterday morning, Green* . . . : "Murder of Jno. Green," *San Antonio Daily Express,* 7/11/1873, p. 3.

127. *on the relief* . . . : Ibid.

128. *The court has* . . . : *Gabriel W. Marnoch v. The United States and the Kickapoo, Comanche, and Kiowa Indians,* #3709, Brief regarding three depositions, the Court of Claims of the United States, Indian Depredations, Filed 7-25-1916.

128. *considered not sound* . . . ; *committed suicide:* San Antonio Daily *Herald,* 7/11/1873, p. 3.

128. *the captain wanted* . . . ; *Americans and not* . . . ; "Because the Mexicans . . . ; *challenged a duel:* Matilde Menchaca memoir, 1/1/1956 (Rogelio Robles Collection).

129. *feloniously, willfully and* . . . : Indictment, *The State of Texas vs. Cesario Menchaca,* No. 13766, 5/26/1897, Texas State Archives, Extradition Records, Cesario Menchaca, 1897.

129. *by the hands* . . . : "Letter from Bandera," *San Antonio Daily Herald,* 7/26/1873, p. 2.

Author's Note

131. *I found Shirley . . . :* Michael Cary. "No Rest in Peace: Pioneer buried under front lawn in subdivision," *San Antonio Current*, 9/1/2005.

133. *height 5 feet . . . : List of Fugitives from Justice for 1900*, Adjutant General's Office, State of Texas, Austin, compiled from Fugitive List of 1896 and subsequent reports of sheriffs received, Menchaca, Cesario, p. 10.

133. *disallowed; not contain specific*: Correspondence from American Mexican Claims Commission, Award No. 724, General Docket 1678, Claimant John Green, 6/28/1946. Shirley Green Sweet papers.

133. *the biggest winners:* Larry C. Skogen. *Indian Depredation Claims 1796–1920*, p. 210.

Roster of Texas Ranger Minute Men, Company V, Medina County, 1872–1873

NAME	PLACE OF BIRTH	DOB – DOD	RESIDENCE IN 1872	TERM OF SERVICE
Haby, George, Lt.	Alsace, France	5/12/1830–5/31/1902	Medina County	Sept. 1, 1872–July 15, 1873
Green, John, 1st Sgt	Altendiez, Germany	2/15/1840–7/9/1873	Bexar County	Sept. 1, 1872–July 9, 1873
Wurzbach, Adolph, 2nd Sgt.	Mannheim, Germany	11/13/1840–1/6/1876	Medina County	Sept. 1, 1872–February 28, 1873; April–Aug. 15, 1873
Van Riper, James, 1st Corp	Waterloo, New York	10/14/1843–12/16/1905	Bexar County	Sept. 1, 1872–Aug. 15, 1873
Heuchling, Julius, 2nd Corp*	Saxony, Germany	1847–1920	Medina County	Sept. 1, 1872–February 28, 1873
Beck, Joseph, Pvt	Alsace, France	1843–4/26/1898	Medina County	Sept. 1, 1872–Aug. 15, 1873
Bihl, Frank E., Pvt	Castroville, Texas	3/12/1847–10/28/1929	Medina County	Sept. 1, 1872–Aug. 15, 1873
Boehm, Armin, Pvt	Rio Medina, Texas	9/9/1853–1/27/1914	Medina County	Sept. 1, 1872–Aug. 15, 1873
Braun, Charles, Pvt	Nassau, Germany	12/31/1847–12/30/1916	Bexar County	Sept. 1, 1872–Aug. 15, 1873
Braun, Fritz, Pvt	Germany	10/22/1842–11/19/1932	Bexar County	Sept. 1, 1872–Aug. 15, 1873
Burell, Jr., Joseph, Pvt	Alsace, France	5/1828–3/31/1908	Medina County	Sept. 1, 1872–Aug. 15, 1873
Burell, Joseph Michael, Pvt	Castroville, Texas	3/19/1854–12/23/1932	Medina County	Oct. 1, 1872–Aug. 15, 1873
Haby, Leopold, Pvt	Rio Medina, Texas	11/15/1851–3/9/1929	Medina County	Sept. 1, 1872–Aug. 15, 1873
Jones, Marion Taylor, Pvt	Talladega, Alabama	5/10/1845–10/22/1909	Bexar County	Sept. 1, 1872–Aug. 15, 1873
Karm, John (Jean Baptiste), Pvt	Alsace, France	8/14/1846–3/19/1912	Medina County	Sept. 1, 1872–Aug. 15, 1873
Menchaca, Cesario, Pvt	Santa Rosa, Coah, Mex	8/1831–1/7/1910	Bexar County	Sept. 1, 1872–Feb. 28, 1873; April 1–July 9, 1873.
Monier, Frank, Pvt	Alsace, France	2/15/1843–7/9/1930	Medina County	Sept. 1, 1872–Aug. 15, 1873
Rivas, Francisco, Pvt	San Antonio, Texas	3/23/1830–8/15/1902	Bexar County	Sept. 1, 1872–Aug. 15, 1873

NAME	PLACE OF BIRTH	DOB – DOD	RESIDENCE IN 1872	TERM OF SERVICE
Van Riper, William H., Pvt	Waterloo, New York	10/1847–1929	Bexar County	Sept. 1, 1872–Aug. 15, 1873
Zepeda, Jesús, Pvt	Helotes, Texas	10/25/1849–9/20/1931	Bexar County	Sept. 1, 1872–Aug. 15, 1873
Wurzbach, August, Pvt	San Antonio, Texas	8/12/1851–9?/1934	Medina County	March 11–21, 1873: sub for Adolph Wurzbach; May 1–Aug. 15, 1873
Haby, Jacob, Pvt	Alsace, France	10/10/1833–9/20/1917	Medina County	March 11–21, 1873: sub for Menchaca; July 15, 1873–Aug. 15, 1873; sub for Menchaca
Specht, Fred, 1st Sgt	?	?	?	July 15, 1873–Aug. 15, 1873

*Although muster records (in most cases compiled a few years after service) showed that Heuchling served the entire term, it is likely he was expelled from service as indicated, and August Wurzbach (see below) took his position.

SOURCES:

Ancestry.com: Birth, Death, and Census Records.

Company V, Medina County, Folder 33, 401-746, Minute Men (1872-1877) military rolls, Reconstruction military rolls, Military rolls, Texas Adjutant General's Department. Archives and Information Services Division, Texas State Library and Archives Commission.

The History of Medina County, Texas by the Castro Colonies Heritage Association, Inc., 1983.

Texas Adjutant General Service Records 1836–1935, Archives & Manuscripts, Texas Library and Archives Commission, www.tsl.state.us.

Texas Ranger Indian War Pensions, abstracted by Robert W. Stephens, Nortex Press, Quanah, Texas, 1975.

Wurzbach, August. Affidavit before Notary Public, Medina County, Texas, regarding service in Company V, Minute Men not noted in muster records. July 10, 1919. Velma W. Keller family record.

Sources

ARCHIVAL COLLECTIONS

Academy of Natural Sciences Library & Archives, Philadelphia, PA
Correspondence from G. W. Marnoch to C. F. Chandler, 11/27/1876; 11/30/1876; 12/17/1876. Archives Coll. # 567, Box 22, Folder 7.

Correspondence from G. W. Marnoch to Prof. J. Leidy, 12/29/1876; 1/2/1877; 1/22/1877; 1/29/1877; 2/11/1877; 2/12/1877; 3/10/1877; 4/6/1877; 4/4/1879. Archives Coll. # 567, Box 22, Folder 7.

Archivo General del Estado de Coahuila
5 de Mayo de 1903, AGEC, FSXX, C12, F4, E8, 10F, Múzquiz
Expediente relativo a que se remitió al juez de distrito en el estado, un exhorto del Gobernador del estado de Texas, en que solicita la extradición de Cesáreo [sic] Menchaca, acusado del delito de homicidio.

18 de Mayo de 1903, AGEC, FSXX, C13, F11, E7, 4F, Múzquiz
Guajardo, de la Presidencia municipal de Múzquiz comunica al secretario de Gobierno del estado de Coahuila, que la búsqueda y aprehensión de Cesáreo [sic] Menchaca, originaron un gasto de cuarenta pesos al municipio, por lo cual desea saber si tal nota de gastos debe remitirse al juzgado de distrito o la forma en que debe dársele salida en la contabilidad.

Bexar County Records Archives
Hoffmann, Jacob
Estate of Jacob Hoffmann. Case 8570. Probate Court Records. 3/16/1917.

Marnoch, Gabriel W. and George F.

John Fries vs. G. F. Marnoch, Case 2617, Failure to Pay House Bill, 37th District Court, 1/24/1859 – 4/2/1860.

McClung vs. G. W. Marnoch et al, Case 3785, Cotton Embezzlement, 37th District Court, 8/28/1867–2/23/1872.

The State of Texas vs. Gabriel Marnoch, Case 320, Violation of estray laws and warrant for arrest for failure to appear. 37th District Court Criminal Minutes, Journal A, 1869–1873, 11/13/1871, pp. 182–83.

Marnoch, G. W. et al vs. Braun, Charles, et al, Case 4769. Temporary Injunction granted to prevent sale of livestock owed for back taxes. 37th District Court Criminal Docket, Book H, 4/24/1874, p. 356.

Henderson & King & Leigh & Dittmar vs. G. W. & E. Marnoch, Case 5283. Suit for nonpayment of legal fees. 37th District Court, 11/13/1875–2/21/1876.

The State of Texas vs. Gabriel Marnoch, Case 12. Aggravated Assault & Battery. Criminal Journal, County Court, 8/9/1876, p. 20.

The State of Texas vs. G. W. Marnoch, Case 494, Murder. 37th District Court *Capias* Warrant, 4/4/1878; Affidavits for Continuance, 5/13/1878, 6/13/1878, 11/16/1878, 11/25/1878; Charge, Indictment for Murder, 5/16/1879; Motion for New Trial, 5/19/1879; Bill of Exceptions, 5/30/1879; Assignment of Errors, 6/6/1879; Affidavit for Depositions, 4/15/1880; Subpoena for Wm. Boerner by Jas Van Riper, 4/31/1885; Subpoena for various witnesses who could not be served, 1/3/1887.

Menchaca, Cesario

The State of Texas vs. Cesario Menchaca, Case 783. 37th District Court. Bill of Indictment for Murder, Judge's Docket, October Term, 1873, p. 476. Case Dismissed. Criminal Minutes, Special Term, 1897, p. 331.

The State of Texas vs. Cesario Menchaca. Case 13766, 37th District Court. Bill of Indictment for Murder. Judge's Criminal Docket,

May Term, 1897. *Capias* Warrant, Issued 5/26/1897; Returned not executed, 7/24/1901.

Bexar County Spanish Archives

Bexar County Commissioners Court Minutes
Accounts for horse hire and summoning of jury to hold inquest on the body of John Green. Book A3, Aug. 1868–July 1876. 7/31/1873, p. 416.
Cesario Menchaca appointed Constable, Precinct 2. Book A3, 10/2/1871, p. 257.
Charles Braun appointed Constable, Precinct 2. Replaces Cesario Menchaca. Book A3, 5/27/1872, p. 314.
Resignation of William Green, Constable, Precinct 2. 6/27/1895, p. 148.
Declaration of Intent (for Citizenship). Marnoch, G. W. Book M, 10/30/1886, p. 173.

Bexar District Brands
G. W. Marnoch and G. F. Marnoch Brands. Book B, 2 of 2, April 10, 1860.

Family Histories
Rodríguez, José Policarpo

Blanco County District Clerk Archives

District Court Minutes
Geo J Marnoch. Declaration of Intention. 7/30/1884, p. 275.
Geo J Marnoch. Petition for Naturalization, 9/10/1891, p. 273.
Jno F. Marnoch. Declaration of Intention, 1/16/1890, p. 29.

Catholic Archives of San Antonio
St. Joseph's Orphan Asylum Register of Admittance for Girls, 1873, pp. 42–43. Victoria Menchaca, Josephita [*sic*] Menchaca.

St. Joseph's Orphan Asylum Register of Admittance for Boys, 1892, Francisco Rivas (Jr.), Adolfo Rivas, Martin Rivas.

Daughters of the Republic of Texas Library at the Alamo, San Antonio, Texas
Biography. Green, William F. (VF-Gen) Folder with clippings.
"Coker Cemetery," compiled by Frances T. Ingmire. *Bexar County, Texas Selected Cemeteries (Early Burials)*, St. Louis, Missouri, 1985, pp. 45–48.
"Confederate Veterans of Bandera County and the Sabinal Canyon," Shirley Blackmore Smith, Kerrville, Texas, 10/2004.
"Dr. Frederick Boehme Family History," by Rev. Gerald Boehme, Castroville, Texas, 1963.
"Elmendorf and Related Families," by Wanda Bassett Carter.
Haby Family History.
Map of Bexar, Medina, Bandera & Other Counties, 1879, 912.764; M297-1879.

Eagle Pass Library
Bird's Eye View of Eagle Pass, 1887 Map.
Paso Del Aquila: A Chronicle of Frontier Days on the Texas Border as recorded in the memoirs of Jesse Sumpter. Compiled by Harry Warren and edited by Ben E. Pingenot, the Encino Press, Austin, 1969.

Jersey Archive, Clarence Road, St. Helier, Jersey JE2 4JY (England)
West of England Insurance Company. L/A/20/A Fire Insurance Registers, 6/11/1846–5/10/1850. Insured: Marnoch, George Frederick, 5/24/1847. "Now residing in France . . ."

Kendall County District Court Archives
The State of Texas vs. Gabriel Marnoch. Case 82. Theft of a Mare. Kendall County District Court Minutes, Book A2, 4/8/1875, p. 222.

Mayborn Museum, Baylor University, Waco, Texas

G. W. Marnock file
Note from S. W. Geiser (5/31/1938)
"Collection at Helotes, Bexar County, Texas," by John K. Strecker.
    Copeia, 7/20/1933, pp. 77–79.
List of 212 Specimens Collected by Gabriel W. Marnoch.

The Royal College of Surgeons of Edinburgh Library
College Record of George Marnock. Minutes from the Meetings of
    College Council, 4/21/1826.
"Regulations to be Observed by Candidates for the Diploma of the
    Royal College of Surgeons of Edinburgh, 9/1826."

San Antonio Conservation Society
Elmendorf, Armin. *A Texan Remembers: A bit of biography and some
    incidents in the history of the Elmendorf and Staffel families of San
    Antonio.* San Antonio, Texas, 1974. Copy in Helotes file.

San Antonio Public Library, Texana Collection

Vault
Bird's Eye View of the City of San Antonio, Bexar County, Texas,
    1873 Map.
San Antonio Archival File. Mayors. Campbell, John P.,
    2/26/1903–5/31/1905.
"San Antonio During the Civil War," Thesis by Lois Council Ells-
    worth, 8/1939.
Thonhoff, Robert H. *San Antonio Stage Lines, 1847-1881.* Texas
    Western Press, University of Texas–El Paso, 1971.

Shelf

A Translation of Church Record Book of the Protestant Congregation at Fredericksburg, Texas begun by Burchard Dangers, Nov. 1849. Translated by Ella A. Gold. Gillespie County Historical Society, Inc., 1986.

Baptismals and Confirmations of Santisima Church at Paso de Las Garza's, Medina River. Vol. 1, 1866–1879. Typed and translated by John Ogden Leal, Bexar County Archivist, San Antonio, Texas, p. 12.

Baptisms of Santa Rosa de Lima Church, Melchor Múzquiz, Coahuila 1738–1804. Compiled and edited by Jesse Rodriguez, Los Bexareños Genealogical Society, San Antonio, Texas, 1997.

Baptisms of Santa Rosa de Lima Church, Melchor Múzquiz, Coahuila 1805–1830. Compiled and edited by Jesse Rodriguez, Los Bexareños Genealogical Society, San Antonio, Texas.

Inventory of the County Archives of Texas, No. 86, Gillespie County (Fredericksburg), WPA, Published by Gillespie County, Texas, October 1941.

Knopp, Kenn. *German immigration to America: the Fredericksburg, Texas manuscripts.* 1999.

Kowert, Elise. *Historic Homes In and Around Fredericksburg, Fredericksburg Publishing Company, 1980.*

Leal, John Ogden, ed. *Three Historic Plazas of San Antonio, Texas.*

Marriage Records, Medina County, Texas, 1848–1886. Compiled and edited by G. Mclin, 1984.

Marriages of Santa Rosa Church of Músquiz, Mexico, 1738–1751. Compiled by John Ogden Leal, San Antonio, Texas, 1981.

Rodríquez, José Maria. *Memoirs of Early Texas.* Ed. Federico Martinez. Los Bexareños Genealogical Society, San Antonio, Texas, 2007. (Originally published in 1913), pp. 42–52.

Microfilm

Bandera County Tax Assessment of Land Records

Bexar County Tax Assessment of Land Records

Gillespie County Tax Assessment of Land Records, 1848, 1849, 1850, 1851, 1852

Gillespie County Deed Records

"Assessor and Collector G. C. to Frederick Gruen," 1854–1857, Vol. F, 8/7/1850, p. 229.

"G. E. Co. to J. Luckenbach ass: of F. Grun," 1850–1851, Vol B. 1/9/1850, p. 389.

"The G. E. Company to J. P. Keller ass: of F. Grun," 1857–1860, Vol. G, 12/9/1852, p. 26.

"Wih. & Kath. Arhelger & J. Grun to Lud. Wiemer." Book H, 5/28/1866, p. 491.

Gillespie County Probate Minutes, Microfilm Reel 982775 (30), Vol. A, 1850–1854.

No. 21. "Conrad Ernst, letters of guardianship and administration of the estate and heirs of Frederick Grun, dec'd." September 1852 Term, p. 44.

"Bond and Oath of C. J. Ernst, admin of the estate of F. Grun, dec'd. 11/29/1852, p. 59.

Inventory, estate of Frederick Grun, dec'd, 11/30/1852, pp. 60–62.

Supplement to the Estate of Frederick Grun, dec'd. 12/27/1852, p. 63.

Statement of Auction Sale, 12/27/1852, pp. 63–67.

Petition of Lewis [*sic*] Martin for guardianship of John Grun. 1/1853, p. 73.

San Antonio Daily Express newspaper collection.

San Antonio Daily Herald newspaper collection.

San Antonio Light newspaper collection.

San Fernando Cathedral Deaths, Book 4, 1869–1888. Isabela Rivas Menchaca Death Record #216, 9/14/1870.

Medina County District Court Records
  State of Texas vs. Julius Heuchling. Cases 520 & 521, 3/18/1873.
  Susan Zimmerlie vs. Jacque Zimmerlie, Case 320, 10/7/1873.
  State of Texas vs. F. Beal [sic] *& Sue Zimmerlie.* Case 566 (cont.)
    Adultery. 10/12/1874.

St. Mary's University Special Collections
Colonel Martin L. Crimmins Collection, Scientific Society of
  San Antonio Bulletin, No. 4. "An Annotated Catalogue of the
  Amphibians and Reptiles of Bexar County, Texas," by John K.
  Strecker, 4/1922.
Vance Papers, collection on Henri Castro and his colonists.

Texas Ranger Hall of Fame and Museum, Waco, Texas
Folder on "Burell, Joseph Michael."
Folder on "Burell, Joseph."
Folder on "Green, J. F."
Folder on "Van Riper, James M."
Folder on "Van Riper, W. H."
News Clipping: *Galveston Daily News*, 7/14/1873. "From San Antonio,
  Special to the News," 7/10/1873 (in Green file).
Texas Indian Papers, 1860–1916. Edited from the original manuscripts
  in the Texas Archives. James M. Day and Dorman Winfrey, Texas
  State Library, Austin, 1961.
Indian Depredations in Texas by J. W. Wilbarger. Pemberton Press,
  1967. (Original published in 1889.)

Texas State Library & Archives Commission, Austin, Texas
Minute Men Companies, Medina County, Company V, Haby,
  George, 1872–73, Folder 33, 401-746.
Muster Roll–Texas State Troops, Bandera District, B. Mitchell's
  Company, 2/1863, 401-1292, MR 583.

Muster Roll–Texas State Troops, Company G, Frontier Regiment, Charles de Montel's Company, 2/1862, 401-1300, MR 1619.

Report of the Adjutant General of the State of Texas. For the Year 1873.

Executive Record Book. Gov. Richard Coke. Reel 11. Proclamation for $200 Reward for Fugitive from Justice Cesario Menchaca, 11/25/1875.

Texas Adjutant General Service Records Online 1836–1935. www .tsl.state.tx.us/arc/service/index.php?formType=name.

Texas Republic Claims, Menchaca, Miguel. Files 454-460.

Texas Secretary of State Extradition Records. Menchaca, Cesario, 1875, 1897. Box 2-10/397.

Texas Secretary of State Fugitive Records. Reward Applications. Menchaca, Cesatio [*sic*]. Box 2-10/458.

United States National Archives

Court of Claims, Indian Depredations

Frederick Braun vs. The United States and Kickapoo and Comanche Indians. No. 3045. October Term 1898.

Augusta Ballscheit, Julius Ballscheit, J. A. Green, Mary F. Green, and William J. Green, legal representatives of John Green, deceased, vs. The United States and the Kickapoo Tribe of Indians. No. 7825, 7/1892, RG 123, 16E3 3/10/5, Box 588.

Caroline Huebner, et al, vs. The United States and the Comanche Indians, No. 7821, October Term 1898.

Gabriel W. Marnoch v. The United States and the Kickapoo, Comanche, and Kiowa Indians. No. 3709. Defendant's Objections to Findings of Fact Requested by Claimant, Request for Findings of Fact, and Brief. Filed 7/25/1916.

Chas. Hoffman, adm'r. Jacob Hoffman, dec'd, v. The United States and Comanche Indians. No. 2891. Findings of Fact and Conclusion of Law. Filed 5/28/1917.

The University of Texas at Austin

Benson Latin American Collection

US Dept. of State Microfilm. US Consulate (Piedras Negras, Mexico). Despatches from United States Consuls in Piedras Negras, 1868–1906. Reel 5.

Center for American History

Earl Vandale Collection. "Glimpses of Texas. A Visit to San Antonio," by Edward King, 1874. From *Scribner's* magazine, January and February 1874.

Report of the Adjutant General of the State of Texas for the year 1874/1875.

Report of the Adjutant General of the State of Texas for the year 1875/1876.

San Antonio Notes, Interesting Dates in the History of old San Antonio, No. 2J145.

Transcripts from the Adjutant General's Office, 1870–1876. No. 2Q400.

Perry-Castañeda Library

Map Collection. Sanborn Fire Insurance Map. Ciudad Porfirio Díaz (Piedras Negras) 1905, Sheets 1–7, www.lib.utexas.edu/maps/sanborn/Mexico.html.

The University of Texas at San Antonio

Microfilm

San Antonio Daily Herald newspaper collection

"Indians! Indians!" Letter to the Editor from J. B. Langford, Bandera, Texas, dated 7/8/1873. Published 7/11/1873, p. 1.

"Letter from Bandera." Dated 7/22/1873. Published 7/26/1873, p. 2.

San Antonio Daily Express newspaper collection
"Murder of Jno. Green." 7/11/1873, p. 3.
"It is believed . . ." 7/12/1873, p. 3.

GOVERNMENT RECORDS & REPORTS

Bexar County Deed Records Online. https://gov.propertyinfo.com/ tx-bexar.

Green, John
Deed No. 590, Jacob Hoffmann to John Green, Book U2, 8/17/1868, p. 443.
Deed No. 726, Sarah B. Wood to John F. Green, Book U2, 6/7/1869, p. 542.
Proof of Heirship. No. 358160. Estate of John F. Green, et al, deceased. 3/13/1931, pp. 540–41.

Marnoch, Gabriel W. & George F.
Deed of Trust No. 80. Peter C. Taylor to Gabriel W. Marnoch, Book R1, 10/2/1858, pp. 78–79.
Deed No. 74. Francis Giraud to George F. Marnoch, Book R1, 10/5/1858, pp. 72–73.
Deed of Trust No. 466. Gabriel Marnoch to William Menger, 12/15/1858, pp. 407–408.
Deed of Trust No. 402. Stephen Dannenhauer to Dr. George F. Marnoch, Book H2, 3/20/1860, p. 406.
Sheriff's Deed for sale of Marnoch properties to pay off attorney's fees. Judgment in Case 5283. G. W. Marnoch & wife [actually sister] to W. B. Leigh and A. Dittmar, Book 5, 8/17/1876, p. 155.

Menchaca, Cesario
Deed No. 253. Candido Dias y Sanchez and Lino Sanchez to Cesario Menchaca, San Antonio, 6/30/1856, p. 227.
Deed No. 70, Cesario Menchaca to Nicolas Delgado. 10/10/1865, p. 89.

Texas General Land Office Online. www.glo.texas.gov/cf/land-grant-search/index.cfm.

Menchaca, Cesario. Bexar Preemption, File 000346. Abstract 541. Letter Assigning Helotes property to his children, 6/22/1877. Affidavits of Abandonment, 1/30/1878.

Menchaca, Miguel. Bexar 3rd. File 1117. Patent for 640 acres, 7/13/1852.

Gruen, Friedrich. Abstracts 453-454. File 3681. Land Patent, 11/21/1855.

Gruen, Friedrich. File 3681. Fisher and Miller Colony Certificate No. 787 for 640 acres, Section Nos. 152 & 153, Bigham District, No. 10, 4/20/1849.

US Bureau of the Census

Census Reports for Bandera, Bexar, Gillespie, and Medina Counties, 1850–1930. Accessed online through HeritageQuest Online and Ancestry.com.

BOOKS, SELECTED ARTICLES & DISSERTATIONS

Alexander, Nancy. *Father of Texas Geology: Robert T. Hill*, Dallas, Texas: SMU Press, 1976.

Berlandier, Jean Louis. *The Indians of Texas in 1830*. Ed. John C. Ewers, Smithsonian Institution Press, Washington, DC, 1969.

Bexar County Texas Tax Rolls of 1890. Abstracted by Jacobina Alley & Janey E. Joyce. San Antonio Genealogical & Historical Society, San Antonio, Texas, 2003.

Bexar County Texas Voter Registration, 1865, 1867–69. Abstracted by Jacobina Alley & Janey E. Joyce. San Antonio Genealogical & Historical Society, San Antonio, Texas, 2006.

Biesele, Rudolph Leopold. *The History of the German Settlements in Texas 1831–1861*. Austin, Texas: Eakin Press, 1987 (first edition 1930).

Biggers, Don H. *German Pioneers in Texas*. Gillespie County Edition. Press of the Fredericksburg Publishing Co., 1925.

Brandon, Jay. *Law and Liberty: A History of the Legal Profession in San Antonio*. Taylor Publishing, Dallas, Texas, with the San Antonio Bar Association, 1996.

Burton, Jeffrey. *The Deadliest Outlaws: The Ketchem Gang and The Wild Bunch*. Denton, Texas: University of North Texas Press, 2009.

Cary, Michael. "News No Rest in Peace, Pioneer Buried Under Front Lawn in Subdivision." *San Antonio Current*, 9/1/2005. Accessed online at www.sacurrent.com/printStory.asp?id=60554.

Cazneau, Mrs. William L. (Cora Montgomery). *Eagle Pass: or, Life on the Border*. Austin, Texas: Pemberton Press, 1966. (Originally published in 1852.)

Cemeteries of Bexar County, Texas, Vol. 2, San Antonio Genealogical & Historical Society, 5/2000.

Chabot, Frederick C. *With the Makers of San Antonio, Genealogies of Early San Antonio Families*. Originally published privately in 1937. Reprinted by Paso de la Conquista, Helotes, Texas, 2007.

———. *San Antonio and Its Beginnings*. San Antonio, Texas: Naylor Printing Company, 1931. Reprinted by Paso de la Conquista, Helotes, Texas, 2006.

Cox, Mike. *Texas Ranger Tales*. Plano, Texas: Republic of Texas Press, 1997.

Cude, Elton R. *The Wild and Free Dukedom of Bexar*. San Antonio, Texas: Munguia Printers, 1978.

Darwin, Charles. *The Descent of Man*, Vol. 1, New York: D. Appleton & Company, 1871.

———. *The Origin of Species*, New York: Barnes & Noble Classics, based on first edition published in 1859, 2008.

Day, James M. (comp.). *Texas Almanac 1857–1873: A Compendium of Texas History*. Waco, Texas, 1867.

Dobson, David. *Scots in the American West, 1783–1883*. Baltimore, Maryland: Clearfield Company Inc., for Genealogical Publishing Company, 2003.

Edwards, Emily. *Stones, Bells, Lighted Candles, Personal Memories of the Old Ursuline Academy in San Antonio at the Turn of the Century*, San Antonio: Daughters of the Republic of Texas Library, 1981.

Edwards, Walter F. *Fredericksburg Guidebook*, 1994.

Everett, Donald E. *San Antonio Legacy*. San Antonio, Texas: Trinity University Press, 1979.

Exley, Jo Ella Powell (ed.). *Texas Tears and Texas Sunshine: Voices of Frontier Women*. College Station, Texas: Texas A&M University, 1985.

"Famous Family of San Antonio Peace Officers Helps Make Texas History." *San Antonio Evening News*, 3/28/1924, p. 17.

Faulkner Jr., Frank S. *Historic Photos of San Antonio*. Tennessee & Kentucky: Turning Publishing Company, 2007.

Fehrenbach, T. R. *Lone Star: A History of Texas and the Texans*. New York: Macmillan Publishing Company, 1968.

Francis Scott v. The State. Texas Court of Appeals Reports. Vol. XXIII, 1887, pp. 521–66.

Francisco Garza v. The State. Texas Court of Appeals Reports. Vol. III, 1878, pp. 286–94.

Garcia Jr., Robert. *Ancestors and Descendants of Francisco X. Chavez, Indian Interpreter/Scout at the Presidio de Bexar, 1785*. Helotes, Texas: Paso de la Conquista, 2007.

Geiser, Samuel Wood. *Naturalists of the Frontier*. Southern Methodist University Press, 1948 (first edition, 1937).

Gerhard, Peter. *The North Frontier of New Spain*. Norman & London: University of Oklahoma Press, 1982.

Geue, Chester William and Ethel Hander Geue (eds.). *A New Land Beckoned: German Immigration to Texas, 1844–1847*. Waco, Texas, 1966.

Geue, Ethel Hander. *New Homes In a New Land: German Immigration to Texas, 1847–1861*. Baltimore, Maryland: Genealogical Publishing Co., Inc, 1982.

Gillett, James B. *Fugitive from Justice: The Notebook of Texas Ranger Sergeant James B. Gillett*. Austin, Texas: State House Press, 1997 (first edition, 1921).

———. *Six Years With the Texas Rangers, 1875–1881*. New Haven, Connecticut: Yale University Press, 1925. E-Book, Texas Ranger Hall of Fame and Museum website.

Gold, Ella. *Fredericksburg . . . A Glimpse of the Past. From Logs to Sunday Houses*. Fredericksburg, Texas: Gillespie County Historical Society and Commission, 1981.

Guinn, Frances Reitzer. "Burell descendants, Texas Rangers honor ancestors, former members," *The Hondo Anvil Herald*, 7/25/2002, p. 4.

Gurasich, Marj. *Letters to Oma: A young German girl's account of her first year in Texas, 1847*. Fort Worth, Texas: Texas Christian University Press, 1989.

G. W. Marnoch vs. The State. Appeal from the District Court of Bexar. *Cases Argued and Adjudged in the Court of Appeals*, Vol. VII, 1880, pp. 269-76.

Haley, James L. "Red River War," Handbook of Texas Online (www .tshaonline.org/handbook/online/articles/qdr02), accessed April 29, 2013. Published by the Texas State Historical Association.

Hall, Sarah Harkey. *Surviving on the Texas Frontier: The Journal of an Orphan Girl in San Saba County*, Austin, Texas: Eakin Press, 1996.

Handbook of Texas Online, s. v. "Martin, Louis," www.tshaonline. org/handbook/online/articles/MM/fma61.html (accessed June 10, 2009).

Hatfield, Dot Ferguson. *Grassroots Medina*. 2007.

Hatley, Allen G. *Texas Constables: A Frontier Heritage*. Lubbock, Texas: Texas Tech University Press, 1999.

Herman, Arthur. *How the Scots Invented the Modern World*. New York: Three Rivers Press, 2001.

History of Medina County, Texas, The, by the Castro Colonies Heritage Association, Inc., 1983.

Hunter, J. Marvin. *100 Years in Bandera, 1853–1953* (first edition 1953), Salem, Massachussetts: reprinted by Higginson Book Company.

———. *Pioneer History of Bandera County*. Bandera, Texas: Hunter's Printing House, 1970 (first edition 1922).

——— (ed.). *The Trail Drivers of Texas*. Austin, Texas: University of Texas Press, 1985 (first edition 1924).

Industries of San Antonio, Texas: Its Commercial and Manufacturing Advantages, The. Land & Thompson, 1885. Reprinted by Norman Brock, 1977. Reprinted by Paso de La Conquista, Helotes, Texas, 2008.

James, Vinton Lee. *Frontier and Pioneer Recollections of Early Texas Days in San Antonio and West Texas*. San Antonio, Texas: Artes Graficas, 1938.

John, Elizabeth A. H. *Storms Brewed in Other Men's Worlds*. University of Oklahoma Press, 1996.

Johnson, Melvin. *Polygamy on the Pedernales*. Logan, Utah: Utah State University Press, 2006.

Johnson, Paul. *The Birth of the Modern World Society, 1815–1830*. New York: HarperCollins Publishers, 1991.

King, Emily Brackett. "Early Days in San Antonio Recalled." *Frontier Times*, December 1925.

Kinsall, A. Ray. *Fort Duncan: Frontier Outpost on the Rio Grande: A Sesquicentennial Celebration Edition Compendium*, Maverick County Historical Commission, 1999.

Landois, Jesús Santos. *Músquiz de Santa Rosa, Estractos de la Historia*. Músquiz, Coahuila, 2002.

Marten, James. *Texas Divided: Loyalty and Dissent in the Lone Star State, 1856–1874.* The University Press of Kentucky, 1990.

Martinello, Marian L. *The Search for Emma's Story.* Fort Worth, Texas: Texas Christian University Press, 1987.

———. & Samuel P. Nesmith. *The Search for Pedro's Story.* Fort Worth, Texas: Texas Christian University Press, 2006.

———. *The Search for a Chili Queen, on the Fringes of a Rebozo.* Fort Worth, Texas: Texas Christian University Press, 2009.

Massey, Cynthia Leal. *Helotes: Where the Texas Hill Country Begins.* Houston, Texas: Old American Publishing, 2008.

———. Gugger Homestead. Historical Marker File. Texas Historical Commission, 2008.

———. Marnoch Homestead. Historical Marker File. Texas Historical Commission, 2010.

Maverick, Mary A. *Memoirs of Mary A. Maverick*, ed. Rena Maverick Green. San Antonio, Texas: Alamo Printing Company, 1921.

McDonald, Archie P. *Texas: A Compact History.* Abilene, Texas: State House Press, 2007.

Menger Hotel Guest Register, January 1872–August 1872, Menger Hotel records.

Mexico: Geographical Sketch, Natural Resources, Laws, Economic Conditions, Actual Development, Prospect of Future Growth. Edited and compiled by the International Bureau of the American Republics, Governmental Printing Office, Washington, DC, 1904.

Michno, Gregory & Susan. *A Fate Worse Than Death: Indian Captives in the West, 1830–1885.* Caldwell, Idaho: Caxton Press, 2007.

Miller, Edmund Thornton. *A Financial History of Texas.* Bulletin of the University of Texas, 7/1/1916.

Miller, Robert Ryal. *Mexico: A History.* Norman, Oklahoma: University of Oklahoma Press, 1985.

Montejano, David. *Anglos and Mexicans in the Making of Texas, 1836–1986.* Austin, Texas: University of Texas Press, 1987.

Moorhead. Max L. *The Presidio*. Norman, Oklahoma: University of Oklahoma Press, 1991.

Mueller, Esther. "A Pioneer Wheelwright Shop, at Fredericksburg," *Frontier Times*, September, 1935, Vol. 12–No. 12, 537–542.

Olmsted, Charles L. and Edward Coy Ybarra. *The Life and Death of Juan Coy*. Austin, Texas: Eakin Press, 2001.

Pace, Robert F. & Donald S. Frazier. *Frontier Texas: History of the Borderland to 1880*. Abilene, Texas: State House Press, McMurry University, 2004.

Panfeld, Peter M. *Wild Nights and Roaring Days in Old San Antonio*. San Antonio, Texas: Kothmann Publishing, 1968.

Paredes, Américo. *With His Pistol in His Hand: A Border Ballad and Its Hero*. Austin, Texas: University of Texas Press, 1958.

Penniger, Robert. *Fredericksburg, Texas: The First 50 Years*. A translation of the 50th Anniversary Festival Edition by Charles L. Wisseman. Fredericksburg Publishing Company, 1971.

Pfeiffer, Maria Watson. *School by the River: Ursuline Academy to Southwest School of Art & Craft, 1851–2001*, San Antonio, Texas: Maverick Publishing Company, 2001.

Pingenot, Ben E. *Historical Highlights of Eagle Pass and Maverick County*, Eagle Pass Chamber of Commerce, 1971.

Pioneers in God's Hills: A History of Fredericksburg and Gillespie County People and Events, Vol. I. Gillespie County Historical Society, 1960.

Pioneers in God's Hills: A History of Fredericksburg and Gillespie County People and Events, Vol. II. Gillespie County Historical Society, Fredericksburg, Texas, 1974.

Prewitt, Christa (ed.). *German Immigrant Ancestors*. Austin, Texas: German-Texan Heritage Society, 1997.

Ragsdale, Crystal Sasse (ed.). "Mathilda Doebbler Gruen Wagner," *The Golden Free Land: The reminiscences and letters of women on the American frontier*. Austin, Texas: Landmark Press, 1976, 156–88.

Ramsdell, Charles William. *Reconstruction in Texas*. Goucester, Massachussetts, 1964. (Original publication 1910.)

Reid, John. *New Lights on Old Edinburgh*. David Douglas Pub., 1894.

Revised Statutes of Texas, Adopted at the Regular Session of the Twenty-Fourth Legislature, Austin, Texas, 1895.

Robinson III, Charles M. *The Men Who Wear the Star*. New York: Random House, 2000.

Rodríguez, Rudi R. (ed.), *A Tejano Son of Texas: An Autobiography of José Policarpo "Polly" Rodríguez*, TexasTejano.com, 2002.

Rollins, Philip Ashton. *The Cowboy: His Characteristics, His Equipment, and His Part in the Development of the West*. New York: Skyhorse Publishing, 2007.

San Antonio in the Eighteenth Century. San Antonio Bicentennial Heritage Committee, San Antonio, 1976.

Santleben, August. *A Texas Pioneer*. New York & Washington: The Neal Publishing Company, 1910.

Santos, Sylvia Ann. "Courthouses of Bexar County, 1731–1978," San Antonio, Texas: Bexar County Historical Commission, 1979, www.bexar.org/community/courthouse/courthouse.htm.

Skogen, Larry C. *Indian Depredation Claims, 1796–1920*. Norman: University of Oklahoma Press, 1996.

Smith, David Paul. *Frontier Defense in the Civil War: Texas' Rangers and Rebels*. College Station, Texas: Texas A&M University Press, 1992.

Smith, Thomas T. *The US Army and the Texas Frontier Economy, 1845–1900*. Texas A&M University Press, 1999, pp. 109–10.

Sowell, A. J. *Rangers & Pioneers of Texas*. Seguin, Texas, 1964. (First published in 1884).

———. *Texas Indian Fighters* (originally published in 1900 as *Early Settlers and Indian Fighters of Southwest Texas*), Abilene, Texas: State House Press, McMurry University, 1986.

Stanfield, Jeanette. *The Cultural Development of the Coker Community, Texas*. Thesis presented to the Graduate School of Southwest

Texas State Teachers College at San Marcos, Texas, Aug. 1942.
www.cokercemetery.com/jeanettejones.html.

Stanush, Claude. "Stage Coach Rolled Over History." *San Antonio Light*, 7/16/1939.

Sturmberg, Robert (comp.). *History of San Antonio and of the Early Days in Texas*. St. Joseph's Society, 1920. Reprinted by Paso de la Conquista, Helotes, Texas, 2008.

"Tales of Old Timers." *San Antonio Express Annual Review*, March, 1890.

Texas Ranger Indian War Pensions, abstracted by Robert W. Stephens, Quanah, Texas: Nortex Press, 1975.

"Texas Ranger Memorial Cross Ceremony," *Helotes Echo*, 1/20/2010.

"Texas Ranger Memorialized," *Bandera County Courier*, 1/21/2010.

US Department of the Interior. *Federal Indian Law*. Clark, New Jersey: The Lawbook Exchange, LTD., 2008.

Utley, Robert M. *Lone Star Justice: The First Century of the Texas Rangers*. New York: Berkley Books, 2002.

Webb, Walter Prescott. *The Texas Rangers, a Century of Frontier Defense*. Austin, Texas: University of Texas Press, 2000 (first edition, 1935).

Wilkins, Frederick. *The Law Comes to Texas: The Texas Rangers, 1870–1901*. Abilene, Texas: State House Press, McMurry University, 1999.

Williams, Docia Schultz. *The History and Mystery of the Menger Hotel*. Republic of Texas Press, 2000.

Wright, Albert Hazen and Anna Allen Wright. *Handbook of Frogs and Toads of the United States and Canada*. Ithaca, New York: Comstock Publishing Compay, 1949.

Zagaris, Bruce and Julia Padierna Peralta. "Mexico-United States Extradition and Alternatives: From Fugitive Slaves to Drug Traffickers—150 Years and Beyond the Rio Grande's Winding Courses." *American University International Law Review* 12, no. 4 (1997): 519–627.

FILM

"Edinburgh." *Rick Steves' Ireland and Scotland*. Public Television
Series. 2000–2009.

PRIVATE PAPERS & CORRESPONDENCE

Barrett, Anne. College Archivist & Corporate Records Manager,
Imperial College, London. E-mail correspondence regarding letters between Thomas Huxley and G. W. Marnoch.

Biering, Rodenna. Photographs and information on Gabriel Marnoch and homestead, 8/30/2009.

Boehme, Bradford. "The Jacob Haby I Farmstead," 12/10/1998/
Photographs and information on Burell, Boehm, Haby families,
10/2/2011.

Brauchle, Joseph. Information on Julius Heuchling. E-mail correspondence, 11/16/2011.

Clarkson, Rosemary. Darwin Correspondence Project. Cambridge
University Library, UK. E-mail correspondence regarding letters
between G. W. Marnoch and Charles Darwin.

Cross, Valerie. Information on Van Ripers. E-mail correspondence,
9/6/2010; 1/16/2011.

Dunn, Lori Bihl. Information on Frank Bihl. E-mail correspondence,
9/22/2009.

Elliott, Jean Nudd. Archivist. NARA Northeast Region, Pittsfield,
MA. E-mail correspondence regarding ship passenger lists for
Marnoch family, 12/17/2009.

Farmer, Cindy and Mary Reyes. Information on Zepeda family.

Johnson, Mary Frances Burell. Information on Joseph Michael Burell.

Jones, Dean (Ret. Constable). *History of the Office of Constable and
Contemporary Duties of the Constable*. Orig. paper in Stevie Seitz
collection.

Keller, Velma W. Information on Phillip Carl Eugene August Wurzbach.

Kennedy, Carolyn. Letters & genealogy information from Marnoch descendants.

> Campbell, Anita Marnoch. Letter to Carolyn. 8/7/1991.
> Dreyfuss, John. Letter to Friends. (Undated.)
> Dreyfuss, John. Letter to Jenny and Mike [Evans]. 6/14/1996.
> Marnock, Marvin. Letter to Jenny Evans. 6/10/1996.
> Russell, Bernice Davis. Letter to Anita. 1/24/1994.

Kerr, Steven. Asst. Librarian, the Royal College of Surgeons of Edinburgh. E-mail correspondence regarding George Marnock and school information. 9/15/2009.

LaPorta, Amanda and Jennifer Fauxsmith. Reference Archivists, Massachusetts Archives, 11/20/2009.

Leal, Linda. PhD. Professor of Psychology, Eastern Illinois University, Charleston. E-mail correspondence regarding psychology of orphans. 8/3/2009, 8/4/2009, 2/16/2011.

Mata, Ed. Translation of 1881 Múzquiz Census.

Menchaca, Joseph. Genealogical Information on Cesario Menchaca family from original Mexican civil documents.

Menke, Jim. Information on Castroville Minutemen.

———. *List of Registered Voters, Medina County, Texas, 1867–1872.* Compiled by Jim & Doris Menke. 2000.

Noriega, Candace. Pioneer Memorial Library, Fredericksburg, Texas, Information on *Kirchen Buch* 1865 marriage records, 6/30/2009.

Pagan, Sally. Centre for Research Collections, the University of Edinburgh, Scotland. E-mail correspondence regarding attendance of George Marnock at this university. 9/18/2009.

Pauza, Rick. US Customs and Border Protection, Laredo Field Office. E-mail correspondence regarding International Bridge at Eagle Pass, Texas, 1/23/2009.

Robles, Roger. "Tia Mencha's Story." Unpublished memoir of Matilde Menchaca, daughter of Miguel Menchaca, niece of Cesario Menchaca. 1/1/1956.

Rosas, Ellen. Information on Emelia Menchaca Morales. E-mail correspondence, 8/11/2011.

Saathoff, Wesley. "The Marnoch Mansion." Paper for a UTSA history class. 11/26/1984.

Schmidt, Carol A. Elmer. "The Life of Francisco Vitoriano Rivas, 1830–1902," 9/6/2011.

Schmidt, Constance. Correspondence about Rivas family history, 10/13/2010.

Serrano, Ralph. Bexar County Sheriff's Office. E-mail correspondence regarding nineteenth-century sheriff's ledgers, 11/12/2008.

Sloan, Mary Lee. Hoffmann family research.

Standifird, Beth. San Antonio Conservation Society. E-mail correspondence regarding Marnoch family, 1/28/2009.

Stockley, John. Director, Fort Duncan Museum, Eagle Pass, Texas, 1/6/2011. Information from Windsor Hotel Register and Register of Visitors to the Mesquite Club, late nineteeth century.

Sweet, Shirley Green. Taped Interview with Elvie Green Pyka (1897–1993), 4/15/1978.

American Mexican Claims Commission. Award No. 724.

General Docket No. 1678, Claimant: John Green. 6/28/1946.

Grun, Friedrich. Oath for Naturalization. Gillespie County Court Civil Court, 11/11/1850.

Heirs of John Green, deceased vs. The United States el al, No. 7835.

Indian Depredation. Claimant's Motion to Reinstate (Citizenship Case), 7/31/1917.

Marriage License of John Grun and Auguste Specht, issued 12/28/1868 in Fredericksburg.

"The Greens and the Spechts from Germany to Texas," a brief biography by Diane Hazel, Bulverde, Texas, 2/2004.

Wendt, Fredrick. Genealogical research on Charles, Friedrick, and William Braun.

Zahradnick, Mary E. Death Certificate of Cesario Menchaca, 1/7/1910, filed in Sabinas, Coahuila, 1/8/1910.

————. Genealogical Information on Cesario Menchaca family.

INTERVIEWS

Burell, David. Descendant of Joseph Michael Burell. Personal interview, 5/20/2013.

Evans, Mary Jane. Descendant of Cesario Menchaca. Personal interview, 5/22/2012.

Gibson, William O. Chief of Police, San Antonio Police Department, 1986–1995. Personal interview, 5/6/2009.

Heiligmann, Wayne. Descendant of John F. Green. Telephone interview, 1/15/2009.

Hoffmann, Florence Sachtleben. Haby Settlement, Rio Medina, Texas. Personal interview, 8/3/2010.

Ibarra, Herlinda. Descendant of Cesario Menchaca. Personal interview and telephone interview, 5/24/2006, 6/3/2008.

Kuentz Jr., Charles. Descendant of Augusta Green Robinson Ballscheit. Personal interview, 7/21/2011.

Lampman, Ruth Kuentz. Descendant of Augusta Green Robinson Ballscheit. Personal interview, 10/9/2008, 7/21/2011.

Mata, Ed. Telephone interview to discuss Múzquiz and Sabinas, 2/28/2012.

Menchaca, Joseph. Descendant of Cesario Menchaca. Telephone interview, 8/1/2008.

Morales, Daniel. Descendant of Cesario Menchaca. Telephone interview, 12/13/2010.

Morales, Lawrence. Descendant of Cesario Menchaca. Personal interviews and telephone interviews, 3/31/06, 5/20/06, 11/15/2008, 11/17/2008.

Sweet, Shirley Green. Descendant of John F. Green. Personal interview, 10/10/2008.

Van de Walle, Lorraine. Descendant of Gabriel W. Marnoch. Telephone interview, 8/5/2006.

Wittig, Evelyn Heiligmann. Descendant of John F. Green. Telephone interview, 1/15/2009.

Zahradnick, Mary Esther. Information on Cesario Menchaca. Telephone interview, 5/22/2006.

ONLINE SOURCES & DATABASES

Ancestry.com. *San Antonio, Texas City Directories, 1891–94*. Provo, Utah: The Generations Network, Inc., 2000.

CokerCemetery.com. Coker Family Histories by Bob Battaglia. Information on Marion Taylor Jones and William and James Van Riper.

Department of Public Safety. "Texas Rangers, Historical Development." www.txdps.state.tx.us/director_staff/texas_rangers.

FamilySearch.org.

Findagravememorial.com.

GoogleBooks.com.

Library of Congress Geography and Map Division.

NewspaperArchives.com. *San Antonio Gazette*.

SanAntonio.gov. History of SAPD (San Antonio Police Department).

Texas State Historical Association Handbook of Texas Online. www.tshaonline.org/handbook/online/articles.

Zion Lutheran Church of Helotes History and Cemetery Inscriptions. lonestar.texas.net/~gdalum/history/history.html; lonestar.texas.net/~gdalum/cemetery.html.

Index

About the Author

Cynthia Leal Massey combines her background in journalism and love of history to write award-winning historical fiction and nonfiction history. A former corporate editor, college instructor, and magazine editor, she has published hundreds of magazine and newspaper articles and several books. She was the 2008 winner of the Lone Star Award for Magazine Journalism given by the Houston Press Club for "Is UT Holding Our History Hostage?" published in *Scene in SA* magazine. One judge wrote: "In her exhaustive look at the unique battle over the Bexar Archives, writer Cynthia Leal Massey manages to make history come alive, filled with dark plots and do-gooders of yesteryear, and allusions to cattle rustling and murder and more." The article was also a finalist for the Texas Institute of Letters O. Henry Award for Best Work of Magazine Journalism. Pulitzer Prize-winning *Lonesome Dove* author Larry McMurtry called her novel, *The Caballeros of Ruby, Texas*, "a vivid picture of the Rio Grande Valley as it was fifty years ago [and] a very good read." Born and raised on the south side of San Antonio, Texas, Massey has resided in Helotes, twenty miles northwest of the Alamo City, since 1994. A full-time writer, she is a past president of Women Writing the West.